Laughter

An Essay on the Meaning of the Comic

D1115823

Laughter

AN ESSAY ON THE MEANING OF THE COMIC

HENRI BERGSON
Member of The Institute Profesors at the
College de France

Authorised Translation by
CLOUDESELY BRERETON L. ES L. (PARIS), M.A. (CANTAB)
AND FRED ROTHWELL B.A. (LONDON)

MANOR
Rockville, MARYLAND
2008

Laughter An Essay on the Meaning of the Comic by Henri Bergson in its current format, copyright © Arc Manor 2008. This book, in whole or in part, may not be copied or reproduced in its current format by any means, electronic, mechanical or otherwise without the permission of the publisher.

The original text has been reformatted for clarity and to fit this edition.

Arc Manor, Arc Manor Classic Reprints, Manor Classics, TARK Classic Fiction, The and the Arc Manor logo are trademarks or registered trademarks of Arc Manor Publishers, Rockville, Maryland. All other trademarks are properties of their respective owners.

This book is presented as is, without any warranties (implied or otherwise) as to the accuracy of the production, text or translation. The publisher does not take responsibility for any typesetting, formatting, translation or other errors which may have occurred during the production of this book.

ISBN: 978-1-60450-106-3

Published by Arc Manor
P. O. Box 10339
Rockville, md 20849-0339
www.ArcManor.com
Printed in the United States of America/United Kingdom

TRANSLATORS' PREFACE

THIS work, by Professor Bergson, has been revised in detail by the author himself, and the present translation is the only authorised one. For this ungrudging labour of revision, for the thoroughness with which it has been carried out, and for personal sympathy in many a difficulty of word and phrase, we desire to offer our grateful acknowledgment to Professor Bergson. It may be pointed out that the essay on Laughter originally appeared in a series of three articles in one of the leading magazines in France, the Revue de Paris. This will account for the relatively simple form of the work and the comparative absence of technical terms. It will also explain why the author has confined himself to exposing and illustrating his novel theory of the comic without entering into a detailed discussion of other explanations already in the field. He none the less indicates, when discussing sundry examples, why the principal theories, to which they have given rise, appear to him inadequate. To quote only a few, one may mention those based on contrast, exaggeration, and degradation.

The book has been highly successful in France, where it is in its seventh edition. It has been translated into Russian, Polish, and Swedish. German and Hungarian translations are under preparation. Its success is due partly to the novelty of the explanation offered of the comic, and partly also to the fact that the author incidentally discusses questions of still greater interest and importance. Thus, one of the best known and most frequently quoted passages of the book is that portion of the last chapter in which the author outlines a general theory of art.

C. B. F. R.

CONTENTS

Chapter I

The Comic in General
The Comic Element in Forms and Movements
Expansive Force of the Comic.

What does laughter mean? What is the basal element in the laughable? What common ground can we find between the grimace of a merry-andrew, a play upon words, an equivocal situation in a burlesque and a scene of high comedy? What method of distillation will yield us invariably the same essence from which so many different products borrow either their obtrusive odour or their delicate perfume? The greatest of thinkers, from Aristotle downwards, have tackled this little problem, which has a knack of baffling every effort, of slipping away and escaping only to bob up again, a pert challenge flung at philosophic speculation. Our excuse for attacking the problem in our turn must lie in the fact that we shall not aim at imprisoning the comic spirit within a definition. We regard it, above all, as a living thing. However trivial it may be, we shall treat it with the respect due to life. We shall confine ourselves to watching it grow and expand. Passing by imperceptible gradations from one form to another, it will be seen to achieve the strangest metamorphoses. We shall disdain nothing we have seen. Maybe we may gain from this prolonged contact, for the matter of that, something more flexible than an abstract definition, – a practical, intimate acquaintance, such as springs from a long companionship. And maybe we may also find that, unintentionally, we have made an acquaintance that is useful. For the comic spirit has a logic of its own, even in its wildest eccentricities. It has a method in its madness. It dreams, I admit, but it conjures up, in its dreams, visions that are at once accepted and understood by the whole of a social group. Can it then fail to throw light for us on the way that human imagination works, and more particularly social, collective, and popular imagination? Begotten of real life and akin to art, should it not also have something of its own to tell us about art and life?

At the outset we shall put forward three observations which we look upon as fundamental. They have less bearing on the actually comic than on the field within which it must be sought.

I

The first point to which attention should be called is that the comic does not exist outside the pale of what is strictly *human*. A landscape may be beautiful, charming and sublime, or insignificant and ugly; it will never be laughable. You may laugh at an animal, but only because you have detected in it some human attitude or expression. You may laugh at a hat, but what you are making fun of, in this case, is not the piece of felt or straw, but the shape that men have given it, – the human caprice whose mould it has assumed. It is strange that so important a fact, and such a simple one too, has not attracted to a greater degree the attention of philosophers. Several have defined man as "an animal which laughs." They might equally well have defined him as an animal which is laughed at; for if any other animal, or some lifeless object, produces the same effect, it is always because of some resemblance to man, of the stamp he gives it or the use he puts it to.

Here I would point out, as a symptom equally worthy of notice, the *absence of feeling* which usually accompanies laughter. It seems as though the comic could not produce its disturbing effect unless it fell, so to say, on the surface of a soul that is thoroughly calm and unruffled. Indifference is its natural environment, for laughter has no greater foe than emotion. I do not mean that we could not laugh at a person who inspires us with pity, for instance, or even with affection, but in such a case we must, for the moment, put our affection out of court and impose silence upon our pity. In a society composed of pure intelligences there would probably be no more tears, though perhaps there would still be laughter; whereas highly emotional souls, in tune and unison with life, in whom every event would be sentimentally prolonged and re-echoed, would neither know nor understand laughter. Try, for a moment, to become interested in everything that is being said and done; act, in imagination, with those who act, and feel with those who feel; in a word, give your sympathy its widest expansion: as though at the touch of a fairy wand you will see the flimsiest of objects assume importance, and a gloomy hue spread over everything. Now step aside, look upon life as a disinterested spectator: many a drama will turn into a comedy. It is enough for us to stop our ears to the sound of music, in a room where dancing is going on, for the dancers at once to appear ridiculous. How many human actions would stand a similar test? Should we not see many of them suddenly pass from grave to gay, on isolating them from the accompanying music of sentiment? To produce the whole of its effect, then, the comic demands something like a momentary anesthesia of the heart. Its appeal is to intelligence, pure and simple.

This intelligence, however, must always remain in touch with other intelligences. And here is the third fact to which attention should be drawn. You would hardly appreciate the comic if you felt yourself isolated from others. Laughter appears to stand in need of an echo, Listen to it carefully: it is not an articulate, clear, well-defined sound; it is something which would fain be prolonged by reverberating from one to another, something beginning with a crash, to continue in successive rumblings, like thunder in a mountain. Still, this reverberation cannot go on for ever. It can travel within as wide a circle as you please: the circle remains, none the less, a closed one. Our laughter is always the laughter of a group. It may, perchance, have happened to you, when seated in a railway carriage or at table d'hote, to hear travellers relating to one another stories which must have been comic to them, for they laughed heartily. Had you been one of their company, you would have laughed like them; but, as you were not, you had no desire whatever to do so. A man who was once asked why he did not weep at a sermon, when everybody else was shedding tears, replied: "I don't belong to the parish!" What that man thought of tears would be still more true of laughter. However spontaneous it seems, laughter always implies a kind of secret freemasonry, or even complicity, with other laughers, real or imaginary. How often has it been said that the fuller the theatre, the more uncontrolled the laughter of the audience! On the other hand, how often has the remark been made that many comic effects are incapable of translation from one language to another, because they refer to the customs and ideas of a particular social group! It is through not understanding the importance of this double fact that the comic has been looked upon as a mere curiosity in which the mind finds amusement, and laughter itself as a strange, isolated phenomenon, without any bearing on the rest of human activity. Hence those definitions which tend to make the comic into an abstract relation between ideas: "an intellectual contrast," "a palpable absurdity," etc., – definitions which, even were they really suitable to every form of the comic, would not in the least explain why the comic makes us laugh. How, indeed, should it come about that this particular logical relation, as soon as it is perceived, contracts, expands and shakes our limbs, whilst all other relations leave the body unaffected? It is not from this point of view that we shall approach the problem. To understand laughter, we must put it back into its natural environment, which is society, and above all must we determine the utility of its function, which is a social one. Such, let us say at once, will be the leading idea of all our investigations. Laughter must answer to certain requirements of life in common. It must have a *social* signification.

Let us clearly mark the point towards which our three preliminary observations are converging. The comic will come into being, it appears, whenever a group of men concentrate their attention on one of their number, imposing silence on their emotions and calling into play nothing but their intelligence. What, now, is the particular point on which their attention will have to be concentrated, and what will here be the function of intelligence? To reply to these questions will be at once to come to closer grips with the problem. But here a few examples have become indispensable.

II

A man, running along the street, stumbles and falls; the passers-by burst out laughing. They would not laugh at him, I imagine, could they suppose that the whim had suddenly seized him to sit down on the ground. They laugh because his sitting down is involuntary.

Consequently, it is not his sudden change of attitude that raises a laugh, but rather the involuntary element in this change, – his clumsiness, in fact. Perhaps there was a stone on the road. He should have altered his pace or avoided the obstacle. Instead of that, through lack of elasticity, through absentmindedness and a kind of physical obstinacy, *as a result, in fact, of rigidity or of momentum*, the muscles continued to perform the same movement when the circumstances of the case called for something else. That is the reason of the man's fall, and also of the people's laughter.

Now, take the case of a person who attends to the petty occupations of his everyday life with mathematical precision. The objects around him, however, have all been tampered with by a mischievous wag, the result being that when he dips his pen into the inkstand he draws it out all covered with mud, when he fancies he is sitting down on a solid chair he finds himself sprawling on the floor, in a word his actions are all topsy-turvy or mere beating the air, while in every case the effect is invariably one of momentum. Habit has given the impulse: what was wanted was to check the movement or deflect it. He did nothing of the sort, but continued like a machine in the same straight line. The victim, then, of a practical joke is in a position similar to that of a runner who falls, – he is comic for the same reason. The laughable element in both cases consists of a certain *mechanical inelasticity*, just where one would expect to find the wide-awake adaptability and the living pliableness of a human being. The only difference in the two cases is that the former happened of itself, whilst the latter was obtained artificially. In the first instance, the passer-by does nothing but look on, but in the second the mischievous wag intervenes.

All the same, in both cases the result has been brought about by an external circumstance. The comic is therefore accidental: it remains, so to speak, in superficial contact with the person. How is it to penetrate within? The necessary conditions will be fulfilled when mechanical rigidity no longer requires for its manifestation a stumbling-block which either the hazard of circumstance or human knavery has set in its way, but extracts by natural processes, from its own store, an inexhaustible series of opportunities for externally revealing its presence. Suppose, then, we imagine a mind always thinking of what it has just done and never of what it is doing, like a song which lags behind its accompaniment. Let us try to picture to ourselves a certain inborn lack of elasticity of both senses and intelligence, which brings it to pass that we continue to see what is no longer visible, to hear what is no longer audible, to say what is no longer to the point: in short, to adapt ourselves to a past and therefore imaginary situation, when we ought to be shaping our conduct in accordance with the reality which is present. This time the comic will take up its abode in the person himself; it is the person who will supply it with everything – matter and form, cause and opportunity. Is it then surprising that the absent-minded individual – for this is the character we have just been describing – has usually fired the imagination of comic authors? When La Bruyere came across this particular type, he realised, on analysing it, that he had got hold of a recipe for the wholesale manufacture of comic effects. As a matter of fact he overdid it, and gave us far too lengthy and detailed a description of Menalque, coming back to his subject, dwelling and expatiating on it beyond all bounds. The very facility of the subject fascinated him. Absentmindedness, indeed, is not perhaps the actual fountain-head of the comic, but surely it is contiguous to a certain stream of facts and fancies which flows straight from the fountain-head. It is situated, so to say, on one of the great natural watersheds of laughter.

Now, the effect of absentmindedness may gather strength in its turn. There is a general law, the first example of which we have just encountered, and which we will formulate in the following terms: when a certain comic effect has its origin in a certain cause, the more natural we regard the cause to be, the more comic shall we find the effect. Even now we laugh at absentmindedness when presented to us as a simple fact. Still more laughable will be the absentmindedness we have seen springing up and growing before our very eyes, with whose origin we are acquainted and whose life-history we can reconstruct. To choose a definite example: suppose a man has taken to reading nothing but romances of love and chivalry. Attracted and fascinated by his heroes, his thoughts and intentions gradually turn more and more towards them, till one fine day we find him walking among us like a somnambulist. His actions are distractions. But then his distractions can be traced back to a definite, positive cause. They are no longer cases of *absence* of mind, pure and simple; they find their explanation in the *presence* of the individual in quite definite, though imaginary, surroundings. Doubtless a fall is always a fall, but it is one thing to tumble into a well because you were looking anywhere but in front of you, it is quite another thing to fall into it because you were intent upon a star. It was certainly a star at which Don Quixote was gazing. How profound is the comic element in the over-romantic, Utopian bent of mind! And yet, if you reintroduce the idea of absentmindedness, which acts as a go-between, you will see this profound comic element uniting with the most superficial type. Yes, indeed, these whimsical wild enthusiasts, these madmen who are yet so strangely reasonable, excite us to laughter by playing on the same chords within ourselves, by setting in motion the same inner mechanism, as does the victim of a practical joke or the passer-by who slips down in the street. They, too, are runners who fall and simple souls who are being hoaxed – runners after the ideal who stumble over realities, child-like dreamers for whom life delights to lie in wait. But, above all, they are past-masters in absentmindedness, with this superiority over their fellows that their absentmindedness is systematic and organised around one central idea, and that their mishaps are also quite coherent, thanks to the inexorable logic which reality applies to the correction of dreams, so that they kindle in those around them, by a series of cumulative effects, a hilarity capable of unlimited expansion.

Now, let us go a little further. Might not certain vices have the same relation to character that the rigidity of a fixed idea has to intellect? Whether as a moral kink or a crooked twist given to the will, vice has often the appearance of a curvature of the soul. Doubtless there are vices into which the soul plunges deeply with all its pregnant potency, which it rejuvenates and drags along with it into a moving circle of reincarnations. Those are tragic vices. But the vice capable of making us comic is, on the contrary, that which is brought from without, like a ready-made frame into which we are to step. It lends us its own rigidity instead of borrowing from us our flexibility. We do not render it more complicated; on the contrary, it simplifies us. Here, as we shall see later on in the concluding section of this study, lies the essential difference between comedy and drama. A drama, even when portraying passions or vices that bear a name, so completely incorporates them in the person that their names are forgotten, their general characteristics effaced, and we no longer think of them at all, but rather of the person in whom they are assimilated; hence, the title of a drama can seldom be anything else than a proper noun. On the other hand, many comedies have a common noun as their title: l'Avare, le Joueur, etc. Were you asked to think of a play capable of being called le Jaloux, for instance, you would find that Sganarelle or George Dandin would occur to your mind, but not Othello: le Jaloux could only be the title of a comedy. The reason is that, however intimately vice, when comic, is associated with persons, it none the less retains its simple, independent existence, it remains the central character, present though invisible, to which the characters in flesh and blood on the stage are attached. At times it delights in dragging them down with its own weight and making them share in its tumbles. More frequently, however, it plays on them as on an instrument or pulls the strings as though they were puppets. Look closely: you will find that the art of the comic poet consists in making us so well acquainted with the particular vice, in introducing us, the spectators, to such a degree of intimacy with it, that in the end we get hold of some of the strings of the marionette with which he is playing, and actually work them ourselves; this it is that explains part of the pleasure we feel. Here, too, it is really a kind of automatism that makes us laugh – an automatism, as we have already remarked, closely akin to mere absentmindedness. To realise this more fully, it need only be noted that a comic character is generally comic in proportion to his ignorance of himself. The comic person is unconscious. As though wearing the ring of Gyges with reverse effect, he becomes invisible to himself while remaining visible to all the world.

A character in a tragedy will make no change in his conduct because he will know how it is judged by us; he may continue therein, even though fully conscious of what he is and feeling keenly the horror he inspires in us. But a defect that is ridiculous, as soon as it feels itself to be so, endeavours to modify itself, or at least to appear as though it did. Were Harpagon to see us laugh at his miserliness, I do not say that he would get rid of it, but he would either show it less or show it differently. Indeed, it is in this sense only that laughter "corrects men's manners." It makes us at once endeavour to appear what we ought to be, what some day we shall perhaps end in being.

It is unnecessary to carry this analysis any further. From the runner who falls to the simpleton who is hoaxed, from a state of being hoaxed to one of absentmindedness, from absentmindedness to wild enthusiasm, from wild enthusiasm to various distortions of character and will, we have followed the line of progress along which the comic becomes more and more deeply imbedded in the person, yet without ceasing, in its subtler manifestations, to recall to us some trace of what we noticed in its grosser forms, an effect of automatism and of inelasticity. Now we can obtain a first glimpse – a distant one, it is true, and still hazy and confused – of the laughable side of human nature and of the ordinary function of laughter.

What life and society require of each of us is a constantly alert attention that discerns the outlines of the present situation, together with a certain elasticity of mind and body to enable us to adapt ourselves in consequence. *tension* and *elasticity* are two forces, mutually complementary, which life brings into play. If these two forces are lacking in the body to any considerable extent, we have sickness and infirmity and accidents of every kind. If they are lacking in the mind, we find every degree of mental deficiency, every variety of insanity. Finally, if they are lacking in the character, we have cases of the gravest inadaptability to social life, which are the sources of misery and at times the causes of crime. Once these elements of inferiority that affect the serious side of existence are removed – and they tend to eliminate themselves in what has been called the struggle for life – the person can live, and that in common with other persons. But society asks for something more; it is not satisfied with simply living, it insists on living well. What it now has to dread is that each one of us, content with paying attention to what affects the essentials of life, will, so far as the rest is concerned, give way to the easy automatism of acquired habits. Another thing it must fear is that the members of whom it is made up, instead of aiming after an increasingly delicate adjustment of wills which will fit more and more perfectly into one another, will confine themselves to respecting simply the fundamental conditions of this adjustment: a cut-and-dried agreement among the persons will not satisfy it, it insists on a constant striving after reciprocal adaptation. Society will therefore be suspicious of all *inelasticity* of character, of mind and even of body, because it is the possible sign of a slumbering activity as well as of an activity with separatist tendencies, that inclines to swerve from the common centre round which society gravitates: in short, because it is the sign of an eccentricity. And yet, society cannot intervene at this stage by material repression, since it is not affected in a material fashion. It is confronted with something that makes it uneasy, but only as a symptom – scarcely a threat, at the very most a gesture. A gesture, therefore, will be its reply. Laughter must be something of this kind, a sort of *social gesture*. By the fear which it inspires, it restrains eccentricity, keeps constantly awake and in mutual contact certain activities of a secondary order which might retire into their shell and go to sleep, and, in short, softens down whatever the surface of the social body may retain of mechanical inelasticity. Laughter, then, does not belong to the province of esthetics alone, since unconsciously (and even immorally in many particular instances) it pursues a utilitarian aim of general improvement. And yet there is something esthetic about it, since the comic comes into being just when society and the individual, freed from the worry of self-preservation, begin to regard themselves as works of art. In a word, if a circle be drawn round those actions and dispositions – implied in individual or social life – to which their natural consequences bring their own penalties, there remains outside this sphere of emotion and struggle – and within a neutral zone in which man simply exposes himself to man's curiosity – a certain rigidity of body, mind and character, that society would still like to get rid of in order to obtain from its members the greatest possible degree of elasticity and sociability. This rigidity is the comic, and laughter is its corrective.

Still, we must not accept this formula as a definition of the comic. It is suitable only for cases that are elementary, theoretical and perfect, in which the comic is free from all adulteration. Nor do we offer it, either, as an explanation. We prefer to make it, if you will, the leitmotiv which is to accompany all our explanations. We must ever keep it in mind, though without dwelling on it too much, somewhat as a skilful fencer must think of the discontinuous movements of the lesson whilst his body is given up to the continuity of the fencing-match. We will now endeavour to reconstruct the sequence of comic forms, taking up again the thread that leads from the horseplay of a clown up to the most refined effects of comedy, following this thread in its often unforeseen windings, halting at intervals to look around, and finally getting back, if possible, to the point at which the thread is dangling and where we shall perhaps find – since the comic oscillates between life and art – the general relation that art bears to life.

III

Let us begin at the simplest point. What is a comic physiognomy? Where does a ridiculous expression of the face come from? And what is, in this case, the distinction between the comic and the ugly? Thus stated, the question could scarcely be answered in any other than an arbitrary fashion. Simple though it may appear, it is, even now, too subtle to allow of a direct attack. We should have to begin with a definition of ugliness, and then discover what addition the comic makes to it; now, ugliness is not much easier to analyse than is beauty. However, we will employ an artifice which will often stand us in good stead. We will exaggerate the problem, so to speak, by magnifying the effect to the point of making the cause visible. Suppose, then, we intensify ugliness to the point of deformity, and study the transition from the deformed to the ridiculous.

Now, certain deformities undoubtedly possess over others the sorry privilege of causing some persons to laugh; some hunchbacks, for instance, will excite laughter. Without at this point entering into useless details, we will simply ask the reader to think of a number of deformities, and then to divide them into two groups: on the one hand, those which nature has directed towards the ridiculous; and on the other, those which absolutely diverge from it. No doubt he will hit upon the following law: A deformity that may become comic is a deformity that a normally built person, could successfully imitate.

Is it not, then, the case that the hunchback suggests the appearance of a person who holds himself badly? His back seems to have contracted an ugly stoop. By a kind of physical obstinacy, by rigidity, in a word, it persists in the habit it has contracted. Try to see with your eyes alone. Avoid reflection, and above all, do not reason. Abandon all your prepossessions; seek to recapture a fresh, direct and primitive impression. The vision you will reacquire will be one of this kind. You will have before you a man bent on cultivating a certain rigid attitude – whose body, if one may use the expression, is one vast grin.

Now, let us go back to the point we wished to clear up. By toning down a deformity that is laughable, we ought to obtain an ugliness that is comic. A laughable expression of the face, then, is one that will make us think of something rigid and, so to speak, coagulated, in the wonted mobility of the face. What we shall see will be an ingrained twitching or a fixed grimace. It may be objected that every habitual expression of the face, even when graceful and beautiful, gives us this same impression of something stereotyped? Here an important distinction must be drawn. When we speak of expressive beauty or even expressive ugliness, when we say that a face possesses expression, we mean expression that may be stable, but which we conjecture to be mobile. It maintains, in the midst of its fixity, a certain indecision in which are obscurely portrayed all possible shades of the state of mind it expresses, just as the sunny promise of a warm day manifests itself in the haze of a spring morning. But a comic expression of the face is one that promises nothing more than it gives. It is a unique and permanent grimace. One would say that the person's whole moral life has crystallised into this particular cast of features. This is the reason why a face is all the more comic, the more nearly it suggests to us the idea of some simple mechanical action in which its personality would for ever be absorbed. Some faces seem to be always engaged in weeping, others in laughing or whistling, others, again, in eternally blowing an imaginary trumpet, and these are the most comic faces of all. Here again is exemplified the law according to which the more natural the explanation of the cause, the more comic is the effect. Automatism, inelasticity, habit that has been contracted and maintained, are clearly the causes why a face makes us laugh. But this effect gains in intensity when we are able to connect these characteristics with some deep-seated cause, a certain fundamental absentmindedness, as though the soul had allowed itself to be fascinated and hypnotised by the materiality of a simple action.

We shall now understand the comic element in caricature. However regular we may imagine a face to be, however harmonious its lines and supple its movements, their adjustment is never altogether perfect: there will always be discoverable the signs of some impending bias, the vague suggestion of a possible grimace, in short some favourite distortion towards which nature seems to be particularly inclined. The art of the caricaturist consists in detecting this, at times, imperceptible tendency, and in rendering it visible to all eyes by magnifying it. He makes his models grimace, as they would do themselves if they went to the end of their tether. Beneath the skin-deep harmony of form, he divines the deep-seated recalcitrance of matter. He realises disproportions and deformations which must have existed in nature as mere inclinations, but which have not succeeded in coming to a head, being held in check by a higher force. His art, which has a touch of the diabolical, raises up the demon who had been overthrown by the angel. Certainly, it is an art that exaggerates, and yet the definition would be very far from complete were exaggeration alone alleged to be its aim and object, for there exist caricatures that are more lifelike than portraits, caricatures in which the exaggeration is scarcely noticeable, whilst, inversely, it is quite possible to exaggerate to excess without obtaining a real caricature. For exaggeration to be comic, it must not appear as an aim, but rather as a means that the artist is using in order to make manifest to our eyes the distortions which he sees in embryo. It is this process of distortion that is of moment and interest. And that is precisely why we shall look for it even in those elements of the face that are incapable of movement, in the curve of a nose or the shape of an ear. For, in our eyes, form is always the outline of a movement. The caricaturist who alters the size of a nose, but respects its ground plan, lengthening it, for instance, in the very direction in which it was being lengthened by nature, is really making the nose indulge in a grin. Henceforth we shall always look upon the original as having determined to lengthen itself and start grinning. In this sense, one might say that Nature herself often meets with the successes of a caricaturist. In the movement through which she has slit that mouth, curtailed that chin and bulged out that cheek, she would appear to have succeeded in completing the intended grimace, thus outwitting the restraining supervision of a more reasonable force. In that case, the face we laugh at is, so to speak, its own caricature.

To sum up, whatever be the doctrine to which our reason assents, our imagination has a very clear-cut philosophy of its own: in every human form it sees the effort of a soul which is shaping matter, a soul which is infinitely supple and perpetually in motion, subject to no law of gravitation, for it is not the earth that attracts it. This soul imparts a portion of its winged lightness to the body it animates: the immateriality which thus passes into matter is what is called gracefulness. Matter, however, is obstinate and resists. It draws to itself the ever-alert activity of this higher principle, would fain convert it to its own inertia and cause it to revert to mere automatism. It would fain immobilise the intelligently varied movements of the body in stupidly contracted grooves, stereotype in permanent grimaces the fleeting expressions of the face, in short imprint on the whole person such an attitude as to make it appear immersed and absorbed in the materiality of some mechanical occupation instead of ceaselessly renewing its vitality by keeping in touch with a living ideal. Where matter thus succeeds in dulling the outward life of the soul, in petrifying its movements and thwarting its gracefulness, it achieves, at the expense of the body, an effect that is comic. If, then, at this point we wished to define the comic by comparing it with its contrary, we should have to contrast it with gracefulness even more than with beauty. It partakes rather of the unsprightly than of the unsightly, of *rigidness* rather than of *ugliness*.

IV

We will now pass from the comic element in *forms* to that in *Gestures* and *movements*. Let us at once state the law which seems to govern all the phenomena of this kind. It may indeed be deduced without any difficulty from the considerations stated above. THE ATTITUDES, GESTURES AND MOVEMENTS OF THE HUMAN BODY ARE LAUGHABLE IN EXACT PROPORTION AS THAT BODY REMINDS US OF A MERE MACHINE. There is no need to follow this law through the details of its immediate applications, which are innumerable. To verify it directly, it would be sufficient to study closely the work of comic artists, eliminating entirely the element of caricature, and omitting that portion of the comic which is not inherent in the drawing itself. For, obviously, the comic element in a drawing is often a borrowed one, for which the text supplies all the stock-in-trade. I mean that the artist may be his own understudy in the shape of a satirist, or even a playwright, and that then we laugh far less at the drawings themselves than at the satire or comic incident they represent. But if we devote our whole attention to the drawing with the firm resolve to think of nothing else, we shall probably find that it is generally comic in proportion to the clearness, as well as the subtleness, with which it enables us to see a man as a jointed puppet. The suggestion must be a clear one, for inside the person we must distinctly perceive, as though through a glass, a set-up mechanism. But the suggestion must also be a subtle one, for the general appearance of the person, whose every limb has been made rigid as a machine, must continue to give us the impression of a living being. The more exactly these two images, that of a person and that of a machine, fit into each other, the more striking is the comic effect, and the more consummate the art of the draughtsman. The originality of a comic artist is thus expressed in the special kind of life he imparts to a mere puppet.

We will, however, leave on one side the immediate application of the principle, and at this point insist only on the more remote consequences. The illusion of a machine working in the inside of the person is a thing that only crops up amid a host of amusing effects; but for the most part it is a fleeting glimpse, that is immediately lost in the laughter it provokes. To render it permanent, analysis and reflection must be called into play.

In a public speaker, for instance, we find that gesture vies with speech. Jealous of the latter, gesture closely dogs the speaker's thought, demanding also to act as interpreter. Well and good; but then it must pledge itself to follow thought through all the phases of its development. An idea is something that grows, buds, blossoms and ripens from the beginning to the end of a speech. It never halts, never repeats itself. It must be changing every moment, for to cease to change would be to cease to live. Then let gesture display a like animation! Let it accept the fundamental law of life, which is the complete negation of repetition! But I find that a certain movement of head or arm, a movement always the same, seems to return at regular intervals. If I notice it and it succeeds in diverting my attention, if I wait for it to occur and it occurs when I expect it, then involuntarily I laugh. Why? Because I now have before me a machine that works automatically. This is no longer life, it is automatism established in life and imitating it. It belongs to the comic.

This is also the reason why gestures, at which we never dreamt of laughing, become laughable when imitated by another individual. The most elaborate explanations have been offered for this extremely simple fact. A little reflection, however, will show that our mental state is ever changing, and that if our gestures faithfully followed these inner movements, if they were as fully alive as we, they would never repeat themselves, and so would keep imitation at bay. We begin, then, to become imitable only when we cease to be ourselves. I mean our gestures can only be imitated in their mechanical uniformity, and therefore exactly in what is alien to our living personality. To imitate any one is to bring out the element of automatism he has allowed to creep into his person. And as this is the very essence of the ludicrous, it is no wonder that imitation gives rise to laughter.

Still, if the imitation of gestures is intrinsically laughable, it will become even more so when it busies itself in deflecting them, though without altering their form, towards some mechanical occupation, such as sawing wood, striking on an anvil, or tugging away at an imaginary bell-rope. Not that vulgarity is the essence of the comic, – although certainly it is to some extent an ingredient, – but rather that the incriminated gesture seems more frankly mechanical when it can be connected with a simple operation, as though it were intentionally mechanical. To suggest this mechanical interpretation ought to be one of the favourite devices of parody. We have reached this result through deduction, but I imagine clowns have long had an intuition of the fact.

This seems to me the solution of the little riddle propounded by Pascal in one passage of his Thoughts: "Two faces that are alike, although neither of them excites laughter by itself, make us laugh when together, on account of their likeness." It might just as well be said: "The gestures of a public speaker, no one of which is laughable by itself, excite laughter by their repetition." The truth is that a really living life should never repeat itself. Wherever there is repetition or complete similarity, we always suspect some mechanism at work behind the living. Analyse the impression you get from two faces that are too much alike, and you will find that you are thinking of two copies cast in the same mould, or two impressions of the same seal, or two reproductions of the same negative, – in a word, of some manufacturing process or other. This deflection of life towards the mechanical is here the real cause of laughter.

And laughter will be more pronounced still, if we find on the stage not merely two characters, as in the example from Pascal, but several, nay, as great a number as possible, the image of one another, who come and go, dance and gesticulate together, simultaneously striking the same attitudes and tossing their arms about in the same manner. This time, we distinctly think of marionettes. Invisible threads seem to us to be joining arms to arms, legs to legs, each muscle in one face to its fellow-muscle in the other: by reason of the absolute uniformity which prevails, the very litheness of the bodies seems to stiffen as we gaze, and the actors themselves seem transformed into automata. Such, at least, appears to be the artifice underlying this somewhat obvious form of amusement. I daresay the performers have never read Pascal, but what they do is merely to realise to the full the suggestions contained in Pascal's words. If, as is undoubtedly the case, laughter is caused in the second instance by the hallucination of a mechanical effect, it must already have been so, though in more subtle fashion, in the first.

Continuing along this path, we dimly perceive the increasingly important and far-reaching consequences of the law we have just stated. We faintly catch still more fugitive glimpses of mechanical effects, glimpses suggested by man's complex actions, no longer merely by his gestures. We instinctively feel that the usual devices of comedy, the periodical repetition of a word or a scene, the systematic inversion of the parts, the geometrical development of a farcical misunderstanding, and many other stage contrivances, must derive their comic force from the same source, – the art of the playwright probably consisting in setting before us an obvious clockwork arrangement of human events, while carefully preserving an outward aspect of probability and thereby retaining something of the suppleness of life. But we must not forestall results which will be duly disclosed in the course of our analysis.

V

Before going further, let us halt a moment and glance around. As we hinted at the outset of this study, it would be idle to attempt to derive every comic effect from one simple formula. The formula exists well enough in a certain sense, but its development does not follow a straightforward course. What I mean is that the process of deduction ought from time to time to stop and study certain culminating effects, and that these effects each appear as models round which new effects resembling them take their places in a circle. These latter are not deductions from the formula, but are comic through their relationship with those that are. To quote Pascal again, I see no objection, at this stage, to defining the process by the curve which that geometrician studied under the name of roulette or cycloid, – the curve traced by a point in the circumference of a wheel when the carriage is advancing in a straight line: this point turns like the wheel, though it advances like the carriage. Or else we might think of an immense avenue such as are to be seen in the forest of Fontainebleau, with crosses at intervals to indicate the crossways: at each of these we shall walk round the cross, explore for a while the paths that open out before us, and then return to our original course. Now, we have just reached one of these mental crossways. Something mechanical encrusted on the living, will represent a cross at which we must halt, a central image from which the imagination branches off in different directions. What are these directions? There appear to be three main ones. We will follow them one after the other, and then continue our onward course.

I.　　　In the first place, this view of the mechanical and the living dovetailed into each other makes us incline towards the vaguer image of *some rigidity or other* applied to the mobility of life, in an awkward attempt to follow its lines and counterfeit its suppleness. Here we perceive how easy it is for a garment to become ridiculous. It might almost be said that every fashion is laughable in some respect. Only, when we are dealing with the fashion of the day, we are so accustomed to it that the garment seems, in our mind, to form one with the individual wearing it. We do not separate them in imagination. The idea no longer occurs to us to contrast the inert rigidity of the covering with the living suppleness of the object covered: consequently, the comic here remains in a latent condition. It will only succeed in emerging when the natural incompatibility is so deep-seated between the covering and the covered that even an immemorial association fails to cement this union: a case in point is our head and top hat. Suppose, however, some eccentric individual dresses himself in the fashion of former times: our attention is immediately drawn to the clothes themselves, we absolutely distinguish them from the individual, we say that the latter *is disguising himself*, – as though every article of clothing were not a disguise! – and the laughable aspect of fashion comes out of the shadow into the light.

Here we are beginning to catch a faint glimpse of the highly intricate difficulties raised by this problem of the comic. One of the reasons that must have given rise to many erroneous or unsatisfactory theories of laughter is that many things are comic de jure without being comic de facto, the continuity of custom having deadened within them the comic quality. A sudden dissolution of continuity is needed, a break with fashion, for this quality to revive. Hence the impression that this dissolution of continuity is the parent of the comic, whereas all it does is to bring it to our notice. Hence, again, the explanation of laughter by surprise, contrast, etc., definitions which would equally apply to a host of cases in which we have no inclination whatever to laugh. The truth of the matter is far from being so simple. But to return to our idea of disguise, which, as we have just shown, has been entrusted with the special mandate of arousing laughter. It will not be out of place to investigate the uses it makes of this power.

Why do we laugh at a head of hair which has changed from dark to blond? What is there comic about a rubicund nose? And why does one laugh at a negro? The question would appear to be an embarrassing one, for it has been asked by successive psychologists such as Hecker, Kraepelin and Lipps, and all have given different replies. And yet I rather fancy the correct answer was suggested to me one day in the street by an ordinary cabby, who applied the expression "unwashed" to the negro fare he was driving. Unwashed! Does not this mean that a black face, in our imagination, is one daubed over with ink or soot?

If so, then a red nose can only be one which has received a coating of vermilion. And so we see that the notion of disguise has passed on something of its comic quality to instances in which there is actually no disguise, though there might be.

In the former set of examples, although his usual dress was distinct from the individual, it appeared in our mind to form one with him, because we had become accustomed to the sight. In the latter, although the black or red colour is indeed inherent in the skin, we look upon it as artificially laid on, because it surprises us.

But here we meet with a fresh crop of difficulties in the theory of the comic. Such a proposition as the following: "My usual dress forms part of my body" is absurd in the eyes of reason. Yet imagination looks upon it as true. "A red nose is a painted nose," "A negro is a white man in disguise," are also absurd to the reason which rationalises; but they are gospel truths to pure imagination. So there is a logic of the imagination which is not the logic of reason, one which at times is even opposed to the latter, – with which, however, philosophy must reckon, not only in the study of the comic, but in every other investigation of the same kind. It is something like the logic of dreams, though of dreams that have not been left to the whim of individual fancy, being the dreams dreamt by the whole of society. In order to reconstruct this hidden logic, a special kind of effort is needed, by which the outer crust of carefully stratified judgments and firmly established ideas will be lifted, and we shall behold in the depths of our mind, like a sheet of subterranean water, the flow of an unbroken stream of images which pass from one into another. This interpenetration of images does not come about by chance. It obeys laws, or rather habits, which hold the same relation to imagination that logic does to thought.

Let us then follow this logic of the imagination in the special case in hand. A man in disguise is comic. A man we regard as disguised is also comic. So, by analogy, any disguise is seen to become comic, not only that of a man, but that of society also, and even the disguise of nature.

Let us start with nature. You laugh at a dog that is half-clipped, at a bed of artificially coloured flowers, at a wood in which the trees are plastered over with election addresses, etc. Look for the reason, and you will see that you are once more thinking of a masquerade. Here, however, the comic element is very faint; it is too far from its source. If you wish to strengthen it, you must go back to the source itself and contrast the derived image, that of a masquerade, with the original one, which, be it remembered, was that of a mechanical tampering with life. In "a nature that is mechanically tampered with" we possess a thoroughly comic theme, on which fancy will be able to play ever so many variations with the certainty of successfully provoking the heartiest hilarity. You may call to mind that amusing passage in Tartarin Sur Les Alpes, in which Bompard makes Tartarin – and therefore also the reader to some slight extent – accept the idea of a Switzerland choke-full of machinery like the basement of the opera, and run by a company which maintains a series of waterfalls, glaciers and artificial crevasses. The same theme reappears, though transposed in quite another key, in the Novel Notes of the English humorist, Jerome K. Jerome. An elderly Lady Bountiful, who does not want her deeds of charity to take up too much of her time, provides homes within easy hail of her mansion for the conversion of atheists who have been specially manufactured for her, so to speak, and for a number of honest folk who have been made into drunkards so that she may cure them of their failing, etc. There are comic phrases in which this theme is audible, like a distant echo, coupled with an ingenuousness, whether sincere or affected, which acts as accompaniment. Take, as an instance, the remark made by a lady whom Cassini, the astronomer, had invited to see an eclipse of the moon. Arriving too late, she said, "M. de Cassini, I know, will have the goodness to begin it all over again, to please me." Or, take again the exclamation of one of Gondiinet's characters on arriving in a town and learning that there is an extinct volcano in the neighbourhood, "They had a volcano, and they have let it go out!"

Let us go on to society. As we are both in and of it, we cannot help treating it as a living being. Any image, then, suggestive of the notion of a society disguising itself, or of a social masquerade, so to speak, will be laughable. Now, such a notion is formed when we perceive anything inert or stereotyped, or simply ready-made, on the surface of living society. There we have rigidity over again, clashing with the inner suppleness of life. The ceremonial side of social life must, therefore, always include a latent comic element, which is only waiting for an opportunity to burst into full view. It might be said that ceremonies are to the social body what clothing is to the individual body: they owe their seriousness to the fact that they are identified, in our minds, with the serious object with which custom associates them, and when we isolate them in imagination, they forthwith lose their seriousness. For any ceremony, then, to become comic, it is enough that our attention be fixed on the ceremonial element in it, and that we neglect its matter, as philosophers say, and think only of its form. Every one knows how easily the comic spirit exercises its ingenuity on social actions of a stereotyped nature, from an ordinary prize-distribution to the solemn sitting of a court of justice. Any form or formula is a ready-made frame into which the comic element may be fitted.

Here, again, the comic will be emphasised by bringing it nearer to its source. From the idea of travesty, a derived one, we must go back to the original idea, that of a mechanism superposed upon life. Already, the stiff and starched formality of any ceremonial suggests to us an image of this kind. For, as soon as we forget the serious object of a solemnity or a ceremony, those taking part in it give us the impression of puppets in motion. Their mobility seems to adopt as a model the immobility of a formula. It becomes automatism. But complete automatism is only reached in the official, for instance, who performs his duty like a mere machine, or again in the unconsciousness that marks an administrative regulation working with inexorable fatality, and setting itself up for a law of nature. Quite by chance, when reading the newspaper, I came across a specimen of the comic of this type. Twenty years ago, a large steamer was wrecked off the coast at Dieppe. With considerable difficulty some of the passengers were rescued in a boat. A few custom-house officers, who had courageously rushed to their assistance, began by asking them "if they had anything to declare." We find something similar, though the idea is a more subtle one, in the remark of an M.P. when questioning the Home Secretary on the morrow of a terrible murder which took place in a railway carriage: "The assassin, after despatching his victim, must have got out the wrong side of the train, thereby infringing the Company's rules."

A mechanical element introduced into nature and an automatic regulation of society, such, then, are the two types of laughable effects at which we have arrived. It remains for us, in conclusion, to combine them and see what the result will be.

The result of the combination will evidently be a human regulation of affairs usurping the place of the laws of nature. We may call to mind the answer Sganarelle gave Geronte when the latter remarked that the heart was on the left side and the liver on the right: "Yes, it was so formerly, but we have altered all that; now, we practise medicine in quite a new way." We may also recall the consultation between M. de Pourceaugnac's two doctors: "The arguments you have used are so erudite and elegant that it is impossible for the patient not to be hypochondriacally melancholic; or, even if he were not, he must surely become so because of the elegance of the things you have said and the accuracy of your reasoning." We might multiply examples, for all we need do would be to call up Moliere's doctors, one after the other. However far, moreover, comic fancy may seem to go, reality at times undertakes to improve upon it. It was suggested to a contemporary philosopher, an out-and-out arguer, that his arguments, though irreproachable in their deductions, had experience against them. He put an end to the discussion by merely remarking, "Experience is in the wrong." The truth is, this idea of regulating life as a matter of business routine is more widespread than might be imagined; it is natural in its way, although we have just obtained it by an artificial process of reconstruction. One might say that it gives us the very quintessence of pedantry, which, at bottom, is nothing else than art pretending to outdo nature.

To sum up, then, we have one and the same effect, which assumes ever subtler forms as it passes from the idea of an artificial *mechanisation* of the human body, if such an expression is permissible, to that of any substitution whatsoever of the artificial for the natural. A less and less rigorous logic, that more and more resembles the logic of dreamland, transfers the same relationship into higher and higher spheres, between increasingly immaterial terms, till in the end we find a mere administrative enactment occupying the same relation to a natural or moral law that a ready-made garment, for instance, does to the living body. We have now gone right to the end of the first of the three directions we had to follow. Let us turn to the second and see where it will lead us.

2.   Our starting-point is again "something mechanical encrusted upon the living." Where did the comic come from in this case? It came from the fact that the living body became rigid, like a machine. Accordingly, it seemed to us that the living body ought to be the perfection of suppleness, the ever-alert activity of a principle always at work. But this activity would really belong to the soul rather than to the body. It would be the very flame of life, kindled within us by a higher principle and perceived through the body, as if through a glass. When we see only gracefulness and suppleness in the living body, it is because we disregard in it the elements of weight, of resistance, and, in a word, of matter; we forget its materiality and think only of its vitality, a vitality which we regard as derived from the very principle of intellectual and moral life, Let us suppose, however, that our attention is drawn to this material side of the body; that, so far from sharing in the lightness and subtlety of the principle with which it is animated, the body is no more in our eyes than a heavy and cumbersome vesture, a kind of irksome ballast which holds

down to earth a soul eager to rise aloft. Then the body will become to the soul what, as we have just seen, the garment was to the body itself – inert matter dumped down upon living energy. The impression of the comic will be produced as soon as we have a clear apprehension of this putting the one on the other. And we shall experience it most strongly when we are shown the soul *tantalised* by the needs of the body: on the one hand, the moral personality with its intelligently varied energy, and, on the other, the stupidly monotonous body, perpetually obstructing everything with its machine-like obstinacy. The more paltry and uniformly repeated these claims of the body, the more striking will be the result. But that is only a matter of degree, and the general law of these phenomena may be formulated as follows: *Any incident is comic that calls our attention to the physical in a person when it is the moral side that is concerned.*

Why do we laugh at a public speaker who sneezes just at the most pathetic moment of his speech? Where lies the comic element in this sentence, taken from a funeral speech and quoted by a German philosopher: "He was virtuous and plump"? It lies in the fact that our attention is suddenly recalled from the soul to the body. Similar instances abound in daily life, but if you do not care to take the trouble to look for them, you have only to open at random a volume of Labiche, and you will be almost certain to light upon an effect of this kind. Now, we have a speaker whose most eloquent sentences are cut short by the twinges of a bad tooth; now, one of the characters who never begins to speak without stopping in the middle to complain of his shoes being too small, or his belt too tight, etc. *A person embarrassed by his body* is the image suggested to us in all these examples. The reason that excessive stoutness is laughable is probably because it calls up an image of the same kind. I almost think that this too is what sometime makes bashfulness somewhat ridiculous. The bashful man rather gives the impression of a person embarrassed by his body, looking round for some convenient cloak-room in which to deposit it.

This is just why the tragic poet is so careful to avoid anything calculated to attract attention to the material side of his heroes. No sooner does anxiety about the body manifest itself than the intrusion of a comic element is to be feared. On this account, the hero in a tragedy does not eat or drink or warm himself. He does not even sit down any more than can be helped. To sit down in the middle of a fine speech would imply that you remembered you had a body. Napoleon, who was a psychologist when he wished to be so, had noticed that the transition from tragedy to comedy is effected simply by sitting down. In the "Journal inedit" of Baron Gourgaud – when speaking of an interview with the Queen of Prussia after the battle of Iena – he expresses himself in the following terms: "She received me in tragic fashion like Chimene: Justice! Sire, Justice! Magdeburg! Thus she continued in a way most embarrassing to me. Finally, to make her change her style, I requested her to take a seat. This is the best method for cutting short a tragic scene, for as soon as you are seated it all becomes comedy."

Let us now give a wider scope to this image of *the body taking precedence of the soul.* We shall obtain something more general – *the manner seeking to outdo the matter, the letter aiming at ousting the spirit.* Is it not perchance this idea that comedy is trying to suggest to us when holding up a profession to ridicule? It makes the lawyer, the magistrate and the doctor speak as though health and justice were of little moment, – the main point being that we should have lawyers, magistrates and doctors, and that all outward formalities pertaining to these professions should be scrupulously respected. And so we find the means substituted for the end, the manner for the matter; no longer is it the profession that is made for the public, but rather the public for the profession. Constant attention to form and the mechanical application of rules here bring about a kind of professional automatism analogous to that imposed upon the soul by the habits of the body, and equally laughable. Numerous are the examples of this on the stage. Without entering into details of the variations executed on this theme, let us quote two or three passages in which the theme itself is set forth in all its simplicity. "You are only bound to treat people according to form," says Doctor Diafoirus in the "Malade imaginaire". Again, says Doctor Bahis, in "L'Amour medecin": "It is better to die through following the rules than to recover through violating them." In the same play, Desfonandres had previously said: "We must always observe the formalities of professional etiquette, whatever may happen." And the reason is given by Tomes, his colleague: "A dead man is but a dead man, but the non-observance of a formality causes a notable prejudice to the whole faculty." Brid'oison's words, though. embodying a rather different idea, are none the less significant: "F-form, mind you, f-form. A man laughs at a judge in a morning coat, and yet he would quake with dread at the mere sight of an attorney in his gown. F-form, all a matter of f-form."

Here we have the first illustration of a law which will appear with increasing distinctness as we proceed with our task. When a musician strikes a note on an instrument, other notes start up of themselves, not so loud as the first, yet connected with it by certain definite relations, which coalesce with it and determine its quality. These are what are called in physics the overtones of the fundamental note. It would seem that comic fancy, even in its most far-fetched inventions, obeys a similar law. For instance, consider this comic note: appearance seeking to triumph over reality. If our analysis is correct, this note must have as its overtones the body tantalising the mind, the body taking precedence of the mind. No sooner, then, does the comic poet strike the first note than he will add the second on to it, involuntarily and instinctively. In other words, HE WILL DUPLICATE WHAT IS RIDICULOUS PROFESSION-ALLY WITH SOMETHING THAT IS RIDICULOUS PHYSICALLY.

When Brid'oison the judge comes stammering on to the stage, is he not actually preparing us, by this very stammering, to understand the phenomenon of intellectual ossification we are about to witness? What bond of secret relationship can there be between the physical defect and the moral infirmity? It is difficult to say; yet we feel that the relationship is there, though we cannot express it in words. Perhaps the situation required that this judging machine should also appear before us as a talking machine. However it may be, no other overtone could more perfectly have completed the fundamental note.

When Moliere introduces to us the two ridiculous doctors, Bahis and Macroton, in L'Amour medecin, he makes one of them speak very slowly, as though scanning his words syllable by syllable, whilst the other stutters. We find the same contrast between the two lawyers in Monsieur de Pourceaugnac. In the rhythm of speech is generally to be found the physical peculiarity that is destined to complete the element of professional ridicule. When the author has failed to suggest a defect of this kind, it is seldom the case that the actor does not instinctively invent one.

Consequently, there is a natural relationship, which we equally naturally recognise, between the two images we have been comparing with each other, the mind crystallising in certain grooves, and the body losing its elasticity through the influence of certain defects. Whether or not our attention be diverted from the matter to the manner, or from the moral to the physical, in both cases the same sort of impression is conveyed to our imagination; in both, then, the comic is of the same kind. Here, once more, it has been our aim to follow the natural trend of the movement of the imagination. This trend or direction, it may be remembered, was the second of those offered to us, starting from a central image. A third and final path remains unexplored, along which we will now proceed.

3.   Let us then return, for the last time, to our central image: something mechanical encrusted on something living. Here, the living being under discussion was a human being, a person. A mechanical arrangement, on the other hand, is a thing. What, therefore, incited laughter was the momentary transformation of a person into a thing, if one considers the image from this standpoint. Let us then pass from the exact idea of a machine to the vaguer one of a thing in general. We shall have a fresh series of laughable images which will be obtained by taking a blurred impression, so to speak, of the outlines of the former and will bring us to this new law: *We laugh every time a person gives us the impression of being a thing.*

We laugh at Sancho Panza tumbled into a bed-quilt and tossed into the air like a football. We laugh at Baron Munchausen turned into a cannon-ball and travelling through space. But certain tricks of circus clowns might afford a still more precise exemplification of the same law. True, we should have to eliminate the jokes, mere interpolations by the clown into his main theme, and keep in mind only the theme itself, that is to say, the divers attitudes, capers and movements which form the strictly "clownish" element in the clown's art. On two occasions only have I been able to observe this style of the comic in its unadulterated state, and in both I received the same impression. The first time, the clowns came and went, collided, fell and jumped up again in a uniformly accelerated rhythm, visibly intent upon affecting a *crescendo*. And it was more and more to the jumping up again, the *rebound*, that the attention of the public was attracted. Gradually, one lost sight of the fact that they were men of flesh and blood like ourselves; one began to think of bundles of all sorts, falling and knocking against each other. Then the vision assumed a more definite aspect. The forms grew rounder, the bodies rolled together and seemed to pick themselves up like balls. Then at last appeared the image towards which the whole of this scene had doubtless been unconsciously evolving – large rubber balls hurled against one another in every direction. The second scene, though even coarser than the first, was no less instructive. There came on the stage two men, each with an enormous head, bald as a billiard ball. In their hands they carried large sticks which each, in turn, brought down on to the other's cranium. Here, again, a certain gradation was observable. After each blow, the bodies seemed to grow heavier and more unyielding, overpowered by an increasing degree of rigidity. Then came the return blow, in each case heavier and more resounding than the last, coming, too, after a longer interval. The skulls gave forth a formidable ring throughout the silent house. At last the two bodies, each quite rigid and as straight as an arrow, slowly bent over towards each other, the sticks came crashing down for the last time on to the two heads with a thud as of enormous mallets falling upon oaken beams, and the pair lay prone upon the ground. At that instant appeared in all its vividness the suggestion that the two artists had gradually driven into the imagination of the spectators: "We are about to become ...we have now become solid wooden dummies."

A kind of dim, vague instinct may enable even an uncultured mind to get an inkling here of the subtler results of psychological science. We know that it is possible to call up hallucinatory visions in a hypnotised subject by simple suggestion. If he be told that a bird is perched on his hand, he will see the bird and watch it fly away. The idea suggested, however, is far from being always accepted with like docility. Not infrequently, the mesmeriser only succeeds in getting an idea into his subject's head by slow degrees through a carefully graduated series of hints. He will then start with objects really perceived by the subject, and will endeavour to make the perception of these objects more and more indefinite; then, step by step, he will bring out of this state of mental chaos the precise form of the object of which he wishes to create an hallucination. Something of the kind happens to many people when dropping off to sleep; they see those coloured, fluid, shapeless masses, which occupy the field of vision, insensibly solidifying into distinct objects.

Consequently, the gradual passing from the dim and vague to the clear and distinct is the method of suggestion par excellence. I fancy it might be found to be at the root of a good many comic suggestions, especially in the coarser forms of the comic, in which the transformation of a person into a thing seems to be taking place before our eyes. But there are other and more subtle methods in use, among poets, for instance, which perhaps unconsciously lead to the same end. By a certain arrangement of rhythm, rhyme and assonance, it is possible to lull the imagination, to rock it to and fro between like and like with a regular see-saw motion, and thus prepare it submissively to accept the vision suggested. Listen to these few lines of Regnard, and see whether something like the fleeting image of a *doll* does not cross the field of your imagination:

... Plus, il doit a maints particuliers La somme de dix mil une livre une obole, Pour l'avoir sans relache un an sur sa parole Habille, voiture, chauffe, chausse, gante, Alimente, rase, desaltere, porte.[1]

Is not something of the same kind found in the following sally of Figaro's (though here an attempt is perhaps made to suggest the image of an animal rather than that of a thing): "Quel homme est-ce? – C'est un beau, gros, court, jeune vieillard, gris pommele, ruse, rase, blase, qui guette et furette, et gronde et geint tout a la fois."[2]

Now, between these coarse scenes and these subtle suggestions there is room for a countless number of amusing effects, for all those that can be obtained by talking about persons as one would do about mere things. We will only select one or two instances from the plays of Labiche, in which they are legion.

Just as M. Perrichon is getting into the railway carriage, he makes certain of not forgetting any of his parcels: "Four, five, six, my wife seven, my daughter eight, and myself nine." In another play, a fond father is boasting of his daughter's learning in the following terms: "She will tell you, without faltering, all the kings of France that have occurred." This phrase, "that have occurred," though not exactly transforming the kings into mere things, likens them, all the same, to events of an impersonal nature.

As regards this latter example, note that it is unnecessary to complete the identification of the person with the thing in order to ensure a comic effect. It is sufficient for us to start in this direction by feigning, for instance, to confuse the person with the function he exercises. I will only quote a sentence spoken by a village mayor in one of About's novels: "The prefect, who has always shown us the same kindness, though he has been changed several times since 1847..."

All these witticisms are constructed on the same model. We might make up any number of them, when once we are in possession of the recipe. But the art of the story-teller or the playwright does not merely consist in concocting jokes. The difficulty lies in giving to a joke its power of suggestion, i.e. in making it acceptable. And we only do accept it either because it seems to be the natural product of a particular state

---

1   Further, he owes to many an honest wight Item-the sum two thousand pounds, one farthing, For having on his simple word of honour Sans intermission for an entire year Clothed him, conveyed him, warmed him, shod him, gloved him, Fed him and shaved him, quenched his thirst and borne him.

2   "What sort of man is here? – He is a handsome, stout, short, youthful old gentleman, iron-grey, an artful knave, clean shaved, clean 'used up,' who spies and pries and growls and groans all in the same breath."

of mind or because it is in keeping with the circumstances of the case. For instance, we are aware that M. Perrichon is greatly excited on the occasion of his first railway journey. The expression "to occur" is one that must have cropped up a good many times in the lessons repeated by the girl before her father; it makes us think of such a repetition. Lastly, admiration of the governmental machine might, at a pinch, be extended to the point of making us believe that no change takes place in the prefect when he changes his name, and that the function gets carried on independently of the functionary.

We have now reached a point very far from the original cause of laughter. Many a comic form, that cannot be explained by itself, can indeed only be understood from its resemblance to another, which only makes us laugh by reason of its relationship with a third, and so on indefinitely, so that psychological analysis, however luminous and searching, will go astray unless it holds the thread along which the comic impression has travelled from one end of the series to the other. Where does this progressive continuity come from? What can be the driving force, the strange impulse which causes the comic to glide thus from image to image, farther and farther away from the starting-point, until it is broken up and lost in infinitely remote analogies? But what is that force which divides and subdivides the branches of a tree into smaller boughs and its roots into radicles? An inexorable law dooms every living energy, during the brief interval allotted to it in time, to cover the widest possible extent in space. Now, comic fancy is indeed a living energy, a strange plant that has nourished on the stony portions of the social soil, until such time as culture should allow it to vie with the most refined products of art. True, we are far from great art in the examples of the comic we have just been reviewing. But we shall draw nearer to it, though without attaining to it completely, in the following chapter. Below art, we find artifice, and it is this zone of artifice, midway between nature and art, that we are now about to enter. We are going to deal with the comic playwright and the wit.

Chapter II

The Comic Element in Situations and the Comic Element in Words

I

We have studied the comic element in forms, in attitudes, and in movements generally; now let us look for it in actions and in situations. We encounter, indeed, this kind of comic readily enough in everyday life. It is not here, however, that it best lends itself to analysis. Assuming that the stage is both a magnified and a simplified view of life, we shall find that comedy is capable of furnishing us with more information than real life on this particular part of our subject. Perhaps we ought even to carry simplification still farther, and, going back to our earliest recollections, try to discover, in the games that amused us as children, the first faint traces of the combinations that make us laugh as grown-up persons. We are too apt to speak of our feelings of pleasure and of pain as though full grown at birth, as though each one of them had not a history of its own. Above all, we are too apt to ignore the childish element, so to speak, latent in most of our joyful emotions. And yet, how many of our present pleasures, were we to examine them closely, would shrink into nothing more than memories of past ones! What would there be left of many of our emotions were we to reduce them to the exact quantum of pure feeling they contain, by subtracting from them all that is merely reminiscence? Indeed, it seems possible that, after a certain age, we become impervious to all fresh or novel forms of joy, and the sweetest pleasures of the middle-aged man are perhaps nothing more than a revival of the sensations of childhood, a balmy zephyr wafted in fainter and fainter breaths by a past that is ever receding. In any case, whatever reply we give to this broad question, one thing is certain: there can be no break in continuity between the child's delight in games and that of the grown-up person. Now, comedy is a game, a game that imitates life.

And since, in the games of the child when working its dolls and puppets, many of the movements are produced by strings, ought we not to find those same strings, somewhat frayed by wear, reappearing as the threads that knot together the situations in a comedy? Let us, then, start with the games of a child, and follow the imperceptible process by which, as he grows himself, he makes his puppets grow, inspires them with life, and finally brings them to an ambiguous state in which, without ceasing to be puppets, they have yet become human beings. We thus obtain characters of a comedy type. And upon them we can test the truth of the law of which all our preceding analyses gave an inkling, a law in accordance with which we will define all broadly comic situations in general. *Any arrangement of acts and events is comic which gives us, in a single combination, the illusion of life and the distinct impression of a mechanical arrangement.*

I.   THE JACK-IN-THE-BOX – As children we have all played with the little man who springs out of his box. You squeeze him flat, he jumps up again. Push him lower, and he shoots up still higher. Crush him down beneath the lid, and often he will send everything flying. It is hard to tell whether or no the toy itself is very ancient, but the kind of amusement it affords belongs to all time. It is a struggle between two stubborn elements, one of which, being simply mechanical, generally ends by giving in to the other, which treats it as a plaything. A cat playing with a mouse, which from time to time she releases like a spring, only to pull it up short with a stroke of her paw, indulges in the same kind of amusement.

We will now pass on to the theatre, beginning with a Punch and Judy show. No sooner does the policeman put in an appearance on the stage than, naturally enough, he receives a blow which fells him. He springs to his feet, a second blow lays him flat. A repetition of the offence is followed by a repetition of the punishment. Up and down the constable flops and hops with the uniform rhythm of the bending and release of a spring, whilst the spectators laugh louder and louder.

Now, let us think of a spring that is rather of a moral type, an idea that is first expressed, then repressed, and then expressed again; a stream of words that bursts forth, is checked, and keeps on starting afresh. Once more we have the vision of one stubborn force, counteracted by another, equally pertinacious. This vision, however, will have discarded a portion of its materiality. No longer is it Punch and Judy that we are watching, but rather a real comedy.

Many a comic scene may indeed be referred to this simple type. For instance, in the scene of the Mariage force between Sganarelle and Pancrace, the entire vis comica lies in the conflict set up between the idea of Sganarelle, who wishes to make the philosopher listen to him, and the obstinacy of the philosopher, a regular talking-machine working automatically. As the scene progresses, the image of the Jack-in-the-box becomes more apparent, so that at last the characters themselves adopt its movements, – Sganarelle pushing Pancrace, each time he shows himself, back into the wings, Pancrace returning to the stage after each repulse to continue his patter. And when Sganarelle finally drives Pancrace back and shuts him up inside the house – inside the box, one is tempted to say – a window suddenly flies open, and the head of the philosopher again appears as though it had burst open the lid of a box.

The same by-play occurs in the Malade Imaginaire. Through the mouth of Monsieur Purgon the outraged medical profession pours out its vials of wrath upon Argan, threatening him with every disease that flesh is heir to. And every time Argan rises from his seat, as though to silence Purgon, the latter disappears for a moment, being, as it were, thrust back into the wings; then, as though Impelled by a spring, he rebounds on to the stage with a fresh curse on his lips. The self-same exclamation: "Monsieur Purgon!" recurs at regular beats, and, as it were, marks the *tempo* of this little scene.

Let us scrutinise more closely the image of the spring which is bent, released, and bent again. Let us disentangle its central element, and we shall hit upon one of the usual processes of classic comedy, – *repetition*.

Why is it there is something comic in the repetition of a word on the stage? No theory of the ludicrous seems to offer a satisfactory answer to this very simple question. Nor can an answer be found so long as we look for the explanation of an amusing word or phrase in the phrase or word itself, apart from all it suggests to us. Nowhere will the usual method prove to be so inadequate as here. With the exception, however, of a few special instances to which we shall recur later, the repetition of a word is never laughable in itself. It makes us laugh only because it symbolises a special play of moral elements, this play itself being the symbol of an altogether material diversion. It is the diversion of the cat with the mouse, the diversion of the child pushing back the Jack-in-the-box, time after time, to the bottom of his box, – but in a refined and spiritualised form, transferred to the realm of feelings and ideas. Let us then state the law which, we think, defines the main comic varieties of word-repetition on the stage: *In a comic repetition of words we generally find two terms: A repressed feeling which goes off like a spring, and an idea that delights in repressing the feeling anew.*

When Dorine is telling Orgon of his wife's illness, and the latter continually interrupts him with inquiries as to the health of Tartuffe, the question: "Et tartuffe?" repeated every few moments, affords us the distinct sensation of a spring being released. This spring Dorine delights in pushing back, each time she resumes her account of Elmire's illness. And when Scapin informs old Geronte that his son has been taken prisoner on the famous galley, and that a ransom must be paid without delay, he is playing with the avarice of Geronte exactly as Dorine does with the infatuation of Orgon. The old man's avarice is no sooner repressed than up it springs again automatically, and it is this automatism that Moliere tries to indicate by the mechanical repetition of a sentence expressing regret at the money that would have to be forthcoming: "What the deuce did he want in that galley?" The same criticism is applicable to the scene in which Valere points out to Harpagon the wrong he would be doing in marrying his daughter to a man she did not love. "No dowry wanted!" interrupts the miserly Harpagon every few moments. Behind this exclamation, which recurs automatically, we faintly discern a complete repeating-machine set going by a fixed idea.

At times this mechanism is less easy to detect, and here we encounter a fresh difficulty in the theory of the comic. Sometimes the whole interest of a scene lies in one character playing a double part, the intervening speaker acting as a mere prism, so to speak, through which the dual personality is developed. We run the risk, then, of going astray if we look for the secret of the effect in what we see and hear, – in the external scene played by the characters, – and not in the altogether inner comedy of which this scene is no more than the outer refraction. For instance, when Alceste stubbornly repeats the words, "I don't say that!" on Oronte asking him if he thinks his poetry bad, the repetition is laughable, though evidently Oronte is not now playing with Alceste at the game we have just described. We must be careful, however, for, in reality, we have two men in Alceste: on the one hand, the "misanthropist" who has vowed henceforth to call a spade a spade, and on the other the gentleman who cannot unlearn, in a trice, the usual forms of politeness, or even, it may be, just the honest fellow who, when called upon to put his words into practice, shrinks from wounding another's self-esteem or hurting his feelings. Accordingly, the real scene is not between Alceste and Oronte, it is between Alceste and himself. The one Alceste would fain blurt out the truth, and the other stops his mouth just as he is on the point of telling everything. Each "I don't say that!" reveals a growing effort to repress something that strives and struggles to get out. And so the tone in which the phrase is uttered gets more and more violent, Alceste becoming more and more angry – not with Oronte. as he thinks – but with himself. The tension of the spring is continually being renewed and reinforced until it at last goes off with a bang. Here, as elsewhere, we have the same identical mechanism of repetition.

For a man to make a resolution never henceforth to say what he does not think, even though he "openly defy the whole human race," is not necessarily laughable; it is only a phase of life at its highest and best. For another man, through amiability, selfishness, or disdain, to prefer to flatter people is only another phase of life; there is nothing in it to make us laugh. You may even combine these two men into one, and arrange that the individual waver between offensive frankness and delusive politeness, this duel between two opposing feelings will not even then be comic, rather it will appear the essence of seriousness if these two feelings through their very distinctness complete each other, develop side by side, and make up between them a composite mental condition, adopting, in short, a modus vivendi which merely gives us the complex impression of life. But imagine these two feelings as *inelastic* and unvarying elements in a really living man, make him oscillate from one to the other; above all, arrange that this oscillation becomes entirely mechanical by adopting the well-known form of some habitual, simple, childish contrivance: then you will get the image we have so far found in all laughable objects, *something mechanical in something living*; in fact, something comic.

We have dwelt on this first image, the Jack-in-the-box, sufficiently to show how comic fancy gradually converts a material mechanism into a moral one. Now we will consider one or two other games, confining ourselves to their most striking aspects.

2.   THE DANCING-JACK – There are innumerable comedies in which one of the characters thinks he is speaking and acting freely, and, consequently, retains all the essentials of life, whereas, viewed from a certain standpoint, he appears as a mere toy in the hands of another who is playing with him. The transition is easily made, from the dancing-jack which a child works with a string, to Geronte and

Argante manipulated by Scapin. Listen to Scapin himself: *"The Machine* is all there"; and again: "Providence has brought them into my net," etc. Instinctively, and because one would rather be a cheat than be cheated, in imagination at all events, the spectator sides with the knaves; and for the rest of the time, like a child who has persuaded his playmate to lend him his doll, he takes hold of the strings himself and makes the marionette come and go on the stage as he pleases. But this latter condition is not indispensable; we can remain outside the pale of what is taking place if only we retain the distinct impression of a mechanical arrangement. This is what happens whenever one of the characters vacillates between two contrary opinions, each in turn appealing to him, as when Panurge asks Tom, Dick, and Harry whether or no he ought to get married. Note that, in such a case, a comic author is always careful to *personify* the two opposing decisions. For, if there is no spectator, there must at all events be actors to hold the strings.

All that is serious in life comes from our freedom. The feelings we have matured, the passions we have brooded over, the actions we have weighed, decided upon, and carried through, in short, all that comes from us and is our very own, these are the things that give life its ofttimes dramatic and generally grave aspect. What, then, is requisite to transform all this into a comedy? Merely to fancy that our seeming, freedom conceals the strings of a dancing-Jack, and that we are, as the poet says,

... humble marionettes The wires of which are pulled by Fate.[3]

So there is not a real, a serious, or even a dramatic scene that fancy cannot render comic by simply calling forth this image. Nor is there a game for which a wider field lies open.

3.   THE SNOW-BALL – The farther we proceed in this investigation into the methods of comedy, the more clearly we see the part played by childhood's memories. These memories refer, perhaps, less to any special game than to the mechanical device of which that game is a particular instance. The same general device, moreover, may be met with in widely different games, just as the same operatic air is found in many different arrangements and variations. What is here of importance and is retained in the mind, what passes by imperceptible stages from the games of a child to those of a man, is the mental dia-

---

3   ... d'humbles marionnettes Dont le fil est aux mains de la Necessite. *Sully-prudhomme.*

gram, the skeleton outline of the combination, or, if you like, the abstract formula of which these games are particular illustrations. Take, for instance, the rolling snow-ball, which increases in size as it moves along. We might just as well think of toy soldiers standing behind one another. Push the first and it tumbles down on the second, this latter knocks down the third, and the state of things goes from bad to worse until they all lie prone on the floor. Or again, take a house of cards that has been built up with infinite care: the first you touch seems uncertain whether to move or not, its tottering neighbour comes to a quicker decision, and the work of destruction, gathering momentum as it goes on, rushes headlong to the final collapse.

These instances are all different, but they suggest the same abstract vision, that of an effect which grows by arithmetical progression, so that the cause, insignificant at the outset, culminates by a necessary evolution in a result as important as it is unexpected. Now let us open a children's picture-book; we shall find this arrangement already on the high road to becoming comic. Here, for instance – in one of the comic chap-books picked up by chance – we have a caller rushing violently into a drawing-room; he knocks against a lady, who upsets her cup of tea over an old gentleman, who slips against a glass window which falls in the street on to the head of a constable, who sets the whole police force agog, etc. The same arrangement reappears in many a picture intended for grownup persons. In the "stories without words" sketched by humorous artists we are often shown an object which moves from place to place, and persons who are closely connected with it, so that through a series of scenes a change in the position of the object mechanically brings about increasingly serious changes in the situation of the persons. Let us now turn to comedy. Many a droll scene, many a comedy even, may be referred to this simple type. Read the speech of Chicanneau in the Plaideurs: here we find lawsuits within lawsuits, and the mechanism works faster and faster – Racine produces in us this feeling of increasing acceleration by crowding his law terms ever closer together – until the lawsuit over a truss of hay costs the plaintiff the best part of his fortune. And again the same arrangement occurs in certain scenes of Don Quixote; for instance, in the inn scene, where, by an extraordinary concatenation of circumstances, the mule-driver strikes Sancho, who belabours Maritornes, upon whom the innkeeper falls, etc. Finally, let us pass to the light comedy of to-day. Need we call to mind all the forms in which this same combination appears? There is one that is employed rather frequently. For instance, a certain thing, say a letter, happens to be of supreme importance to a certain person and must be recovered at all costs. This thing, which always vanishes just when you think you have caught it, pervades the entire play, "rolling up" increasingly serious and unexpected incidents as it proceeds. All this is far more like a child's game than appears at first blush. Once more the effect produced is that of the snowball.

It is the characteristic of a mechanical combination to be generally *reversible*. A child is delighted when he sees the ball in a game of ninepins knocking down everything in its way and spreading havoc in all directions; he laughs louder than ever when the ball returns to its starting-point after twists and turns and waverings of every kind. In other words, the mechanism just described is laughable even when rectilinear, it is much more so on becoming circular and when every effort the player makes, by a fatal interaction of cause and effect, merely results in bringing it back to the same spot. Now, a considerable number of light comedies revolve round this idea. An Italian straw hat has been eaten up by a horse.[4] There is only one other hat like it in the whole of Paris; it *must* be secured regardless of cost. This hat, which always slips away at the moment its capture seems inevitable, keeps the principal character on the run, and through him all the others who hang, so to say, on to his coat tails, like a magnet which, by a successive series of attractions, draws along in its train the grains of iron filings that hang on to each other. And when at last, after all sorts of difficulties, the goal seems in sight, it is found that the hat so ardently sought is precisely the one that has been eaten. The same voyage of discovery is depicted in another equally well-known comedy of Labiche.[5] The curtain rises on an old bachelor and an old maid, acquaintances of long standing, at the moment of enjoying their daily rubber. Each of them, unknown to the other, has applied to the same matrimonial agency. Through innumerable difficulties, one mishap following on the heels of another, they hurry along, side by side, right through the play, to the interview which brings them back, purely and simply, into each other's presence. We have the same circular effect, the same return to the starting-point, in a more recent play.[6] A henpecked husband imagines he has escaped by divorce from the clutches of his wife and his mother-in-law. He marries again, when, lo and behold, the double combination of marriage and

---

4   Un Chapeau de paille d'Italie (Labiche).
5   La Cagnotte.
6   Les Surprises du divorce.

divorce brings back to him his former wife in the aggravated form of a second mother-in-law!

When we think how intense and how common is this type of the comic, we understand why it has fascinated the imagination of certain philosophers. To cover a good deal of ground only to come back unwittingly to the starting-point, is to make a great effort for a result that is nil. So we might be tempted to define the comic in this latter fashion. And such, indeed, seems to be the idea of Herbert Spencer: according to him, laughter is the indication of an effort which suddenly encounters a void. Kant had already said something of the kind: "Laughter is the result of an expectation, which, of a sudden, ends in nothing." No doubt these definitions would apply to the last few examples given, although, even then, the formula needs the addition of sundry limitations, for we often make an ineffectual effort which is in no way provocative of laughter. While, however, the last few examples are illustrations of a great cause resulting in a small effect, we quoted others, immediately before, which might be defined inversely as a great effect springing from a small cause. The truth is, this second definition has scarcely more validity than the first. Lack of proportion between cause and effect, whether appearing in one or in the other, is never the direct source of laughter. What we do laugh at is something that this lack of proportion may in certain cases disclose, namely, a particular mechanical arrangement which it reveals to us, as through a glass, at the back of the series of effects and causes. Disregard this arrangement, and you let go the only clue capable of guiding you through the labyrinth of the comic. Any hypothesis you otherwise would select, while possibly applicable to a few carefully chosen cases, is liable at any moment to be met and overthrown by the first unsuitable instance that comes along.

But why is it we laugh at this mechanical arrangement? It is doubtless strange that the history of a person or of a group should sometimes appear like a game worked by strings, or gearings, or springs; but from what source does the special character of this strangeness arise? What is it that makes it laughable? To this question, which we have already propounded in various forms, our answer must always be the same. The rigid mechanism which we occasionally detect, as a foreign body, in the living continuity of human affairs is of peculiar interest to us as being a kind of *absentmindedness* on the part of life. Were events unceasingly mindful of their own course, there would be no coincidences, no conjunctures and no circular series; everything would evolve and progress continuously. And were all men always attentive to life, were we constantly keeping in touch with others as well as with ourselves, nothing within us would ever appear as due to the working of strings or springs. The comic is that side of a person which reveals his likeness to a thing, that aspect of human events which, through its peculiar inelasticity, conveys the impression of pure mechanism, of automatism, of movement without life. Consequently it expresses an individual or collective imperfection which calls for an immediate corrective. This corrective is laughter, a social gesture that singles out and represses a special kind of absentmindedness in men and in events.

But this in turn tempts us to make further investigations. So far, we have spent our time in rediscovering, in the diversions of the grownup man, those mechanical combinations which amused him as a child. Our methods, in fact, have been entirely empirical. Let us now attempt to frame a full and methodical theory, by seeking, as it were, at the fountainhead, the changeless and simple archetypes of the manifold and transient practices of the comic stage. Comedy, we said, combines events so as to introduce mechanism into the outer forms of life. Let us now ascertain in what essential characteristics life, when viewed from without, seems to contrast with mere mechanism. We shall only have, then, to turn to the opposite characteristics, in order to discover the abstract formula, this time a general and complete one, for every real and possible method of comedy.

Life presents itself to us as evolution in time and complexity in space. Regarded in time, it is the continuous evolution of a being ever growing older; it never goes backwards and never repeats anything. Considered in space, it exhibits certain coexisting elements so closely interdependent, so exclusively made for one another, that not one of them could, at the same time, belong to two different organisms: each living being is a closed system of phenomena, incapable of interfering with other systems. A continual change of aspect, the irreversibility of the order of phenomena, the perfect individuality of a perfectly self-contained series: such, then, are the outward characteristics – whether real or apparent is of little moment – which distinguish the living from the merely mechanical. Let us take the counterpart of each of these: we shall obtain three processes which might be called *Repetition, Inversion, and Reciprocal Interference of Series.* Now, it is easy to see that these are also the methods of light comedy, and that no others are possible.

As a matter of fact, we could discover them, as ingredients of varying importance, in the composition of all the scenes we have just been considering, and, a fortiori, in the children's games, the mechanism of which they reproduce. The requisite analysis would, however, delay us too long, and it is more profitable to study them in their purity by taking fresh examples. Nothing could be easier, for it is in their pure state that they are found both in classic comedy and in contemporary plays.

I.   REPETITION - Our present problem no longer deals, like the preceding one, with a word or a sentence repeated by an individual, but rather with a situation, that is, a combination of circumstances, which recurs several times in its original form and thus contrasts with the changing stream of life. Everyday experience supplies us with this type of the comic, though only in a rudimentary state. Thus, you meet a friend in the street whom you have not seen for an age; there is nothing comic in the situation. If, however, you meet, him again the same day, and then a third and a fourth time, you may laugh at the "coincidence." Now, picture to yourself a series of imaginary events which affords a tolerably fair illusion of life, and within this ever-moving series imagine one and the same scene reproduced either by the same characters or by different ones: again you will have a coincidence, though a far more extraordinary one.

Such are the repetitions produced on the stage. They are the more laughable in proportion as the scene repeated is more complex and more naturally introduced – two conditions which seem mutually exclusive, and which the play-writer must be clever enough to reconcile.

Contemporary light comedy employs this method in every shape and form. One of the best-known examples consists in bringing a group of characters, act after act, into the most varied surroundings, so as to reproduce, under ever fresh circumstances, one and the same series of incidents or accidents more or less symmetrically identical.

In several of Moliere's plays we find one and the same arrangement of events repeated right through the comedy from beginning to end. Thus, the Ecole des femmes does nothing more than reproduce and re-peat a single incident in three tempi: first tempo, Horace tells Arnolphe of the plan he has devised to deceive Agnes's guardian, who turns out to be Arnolphe himself; second tempo, Arnolphe thinks he has check-mated the move; third tempo, Agnes contrives that Horace gets all the benefit of Arnolphe's precautionary measures. There is the same sym-metrical repetition in the Ecole des marts, in L'Etourdi, and above all in George Dandin, where the same effect in three tempi is again met with: first tempo, George Dandin discovers that his wife is unfaithful;

second tempo, he summons his father – and mother-in-law to his assistance; third tempo, it is George Dandin himself, after all, who has to apologise.

At times the same scene is reproduced with groups of different characters. Then it not infrequently happens that the first group consists of masters and the second of servants. The latter repeat in another key a scene already played by the former, though the rendering is naturally less refined. A part of the Depit amoureux is constructed on this plan, as is also Amphitryon. In an amusing little comedy of Benedix, Der Eigensinn, the order is inverted: we have the masters reproducing a scene of stubbornness in which their servants have set the example.

But, quite irrespective of the characters who serve as pegs for the arrangement of symmetrical situations, there seems to be a wide gulf between classic comedy and the theatre of to-day. Both aim at introducing a certain mathematical order into events, while none the less maintaining their aspect of likelihood, that is to say, of life. But the means they employ are different. The majority of light comedies of our day seek to mesmerise directly the mind of the spectator. For, however extraordinary the coincidence, it becomes acceptable from the very fact that it is accepted; and we do accept it, if we have been gradually prepared for its reception. Such is often the procedure adopted by contemporary authors. In Moliere's plays, on the contrary, it is the moods of the persons on the stage, not of the audience, that make repetition seem natural. Each of the characters represents a certain force applied in a certain direction, and it is because these forces, constant in direction, necessarily combine together in the same way, that the same situation is reproduced. Thus interpreted, the comedy of situation is akin to the comedy of character. It deserves to be called classic, if classic art is indeed that which does not claim to derive from the effect more than it has put into the cause.

2.   INVERSION – This second method has so much analogy with the first that we will merely define it without insisting on illustrations. Picture to yourself certain characters in a certain situation: if you reverse the situation and invert the roles, you obtain a comic scene. The double rescue scene in Le Voyage de M. Perrichon belongs to this class.[7] There is no necessity, however, for both the identical scenes to be played before us. We may be shown only one, provided the other is really in our minds. Thus, we laugh at the prisoner at the bar lecturing the magistrate; at a

---

7   Labiche, "Le Voyage de M. Perrichon."

child presuming to teach its parents; in a word, at everything that comes under the heading of "topsyturvydom." Not infrequently comedy sets before us a character who lays a trap in which he is the first to be caught. The plot of the villain who is the victim of his own villainy, or the cheat cheated, forms the stock-in-trade of a good many plays. We find this even in primitive farce. Lawyer Pathelin tells his client of a trick to out-wit the magistrate; the client employs the self-same trick to avoid paying the lawyer. A termagant of a wife insists upon her husband doing all the housework; she has put down each separate item on a "rota." Now let her fall into a copper, her husband will refuse to drag her out, for "that is not down on his 'rota.'" In modern literature we meet with hundreds of variations on the theme of the robber robbed. In every case the root idea involves an inversion of roles, and a situation which recoils on the head of its author.

Here we apparently find the confirmation of a law, some illustra-tions of which we have already pointed out. When a comic scene has been reproduced a number of times, it reaches the stage of being a classical type or model. It becomes amusing in itself, quite apart from the causes which render it amusing. Henceforth, new scenes, which are not comic de jure, may become amusing de facto, on account of their partial resemblance to this model. They call up in our mind a more or less confused image which we know to be comical. They range themselves in a category representing an officially recognised type of the comic. The scene of the "robber robbed" belongs to this class. It casts over a host of other scenes a reflection of the comic ele-ment it contains. In the end it renders comic any mishap that befalls one through one's own fault, no matter what the fault or mishap may be, – nay, an allusion to this mishap, a single word that recalls it, is sufficient. There would be nothing amusing in the saying, "It serves you right, George Dandin," were it not for the comic overtones that take up and re-echo it.

3.   WE have dwelt at considerable length on repetition and inver-sion; we now come to the reciprocal interference[8] of series. This is a comic effect, the precise formula of which is very difficult to disentangle, by reason of the extraordinary variety of forms in which it appears on the stage. Perhaps it might be defined as follows: A situation is invari-ably comic when it belongs simultaneously to two altogether indepen-

---

8   The word "interference" has here the meaning given to it in Optics, where it indi-cates the partial superposition and neutralisation, by each other, of two series of light-waves.

dent series of events and is capable of being interpreted in two entirely different meanings at the same time.

You will at once think of an equivocal situation. And the equivocal situation is indeed one which permits of two different meanings at the same time, the one merely plausible, which is put forward by the actors, the other a real one, which is given by the public. We see the real meaning of the situation, because care has been taken to show us every aspect of it; but each of the actors knows only one of these aspects: hence the mistakes they make and the erroneous judgments they pass both on what is going on around them and on what they are doing themselves. We proceed from this erroneous judgment to the correct one, we waver between the possible meaning and the real, and it is this mental seesaw between two contrary interpretations which is at first apparent in the enjoyment we derive from an equivocal situation. It is natural that certain philosophers should have been specially struck by this mental instability, and that some of them should regard the very essence of the ludicrous as consisting in the collision or coincidence of two judgments that contradict each other. Their definition, however, is far from meeting every case, and even when it does, it defines – not the principle of the ludicrous, but only one of its more or less distant consequences. Indeed, it is easy to see that the stage-made misunderstanding is nothing but a particular instance of a far more general phenomenon, – the reciprocal interference of independent series, and that, moreover, it is not laughable in itself, but only as a sign of such an interference.

As a matter of fact, each of the characters in every stage-made misunderstanding has his setting in an appropriate series of events which he correctly interprets as far as he is concerned, and which give the key-note to his words and actions. Each of the series peculiar to the several characters develop independently, but at a certain moment they meet under such conditions that the actions and words that belong to one might just as well belong to another. Hence arise the misunderstandings and the equivocal nature of the situation. But this latter is not laughable in itself, it is so only because it reveals the coincidence of the two independent series. The proof of this lies in the fact that the author must be continually taxing his ingenuity to recall our attention to the double fact of independence and coincidence. This he generally succeeds in doing by constantly renewing the vain threat of dissolving partnership between the two coinciding series. Every moment the whole thing threatens to break down, but manages to get patched up again; it is this diversion that excites laughter, far more than the oscillation of the mind between two contradictory ideas. It makes us laugh because it reveals to us the reciprocal interference of two independent series, the real source of the comic effect.

And so the stage-made misunderstanding is nothing more than one particular instance, one means – perhaps the most artificial – of illustrating the reciprocal interference of series, but it is not the only one. Instead of two contemporary series, you might take one series of events belonging to the past and another belonging to the present: if the two series happen to coincide in our imagination, there will be no resulting cross-purposes, and yet the same comic effect will continue to take place. Think of Bonivard, captive in the Castle of Chillon: one series of facts. Now picture to yourself Tartarin, travelling in Switzerland, arrested and imprisoned: second series, independent of the former. Now let Tartarin be manacled to Bonivard's chain, thus making the two stories seem for a moment to coincide, and you will get a very amusing scene, one of the most amusing that Daudet's imagination has pictured. [Tartarin sur les Alpes, by Daudet.] Numerous incidents of the mock-heroic style, if analysed, would reveal the same elements. The transposition from the ancient to the modern – always a laughable one – draws its inspiration from the same idea. Labiche has made use of this method in every shape and form. Sometimes he begins by building up the series separately, and then delights in making them interfere with one another: he takes an independent group – a wedding-party, for instance – and throws them into altogether unconnected surroundings, into which certain coincidences allow of their being foisted for the time being. Sometimes he keeps one and the same set of characters right through the play, but contrives that certain of these characters have something to conceal – have, in fact, a secret understanding on the point – in short, play a smaller comedy within the principal one: at one moment, one of the two comedies is on the point of upsetting the other; the next, everything comes right and the coincidence between the two series is restored. Sometimes, even, he introduces into the actual series a purely immaterial series of events, an inconvenient past, for instance, that some one has an interest in concealing, but which is continually cropping up in the present, and on each occasion is successfully brought into line with situations with which it seemed destined to play havoc. But in every case we find the two independent series, and also their partial coincidence.

We will not carry any further this analysis of the methods of light comedy. Whether we find reciprocal interference of series, inversion, or repetition, we see that the objective is always the same – to obtain what we have called a *mechanisation* of life. You take a set of actions and relations and repeat it as it is, or turn it upside down, or transfer it bodily to another set with which it partially coincides – all these being processes that consist in looking upon life as a repeating mechanism, with reversible action and interchangeable parts. Actual life is comedy just so far as it produces, in a natural fashion, actions of the same kind, – consequently, just so far as it forgets itself, for were it always on the alert, it would be ever-changing continuity, irrevertible progress, undivided unity. And so the ludicrous in events may be defined as absentmindedness in things, just as the ludicrous in an individual character always results from some fundamental absentmindedness in the person, as we have already intimated and shall prove later on. This absentmindedness in events, however, is exceptional. Its results are slight. At any rate it is incurable, so that it is useless to laugh at it. Therefore the idea would never have occurred to any one of exaggerating that absentmindedness, of converting it into a system and creating an art for it, if laughter were not always a pleasure and mankind did not pounce upon the slightest excuse for indulging in it. This is the real explanation of light comedy, which holds the same relation to actual life as does a jointed dancing-doll to a man walking, – being, as it is, an artificial exaggeration of a natural rigidity in things. The thread that binds it to actual life is a very fragile one. It is scarcely more than a game which, like all games, depends on a previously accepted convention. Comedy in character strikes far deeper roots into life. With that kind of comedy we shall deal more particularly in the final portion of our investigation. But we must first analyse a certain type of the comic, in many respects similar to that of light comedy: the comic in words.

II

There may be something artificial in making a special category for the comic in words, since most of the varieties of the comic that we have examined so far were produced through the medium of language. We must make a distinction, however, between the comic *expressed* and the comic *created* by language. The former could, if necessary, be translated from one language into another, though at the cost of losing the greater portion of its significance when introduced into a fresh society different in manners, in literature, and above all in association of ideas. But it is generally impossible to translate the latter. It owes its entire being to the structure of the sentence or to the choice of the words. It does not set forth, by means of language, special cases of absentmindedness in man or in events. It lays stress on lapses of attention in language itself. In this case, it is language itself that becomes comic.

Comic sayings, however, are not a matter of spontaneous generation; if we laugh at them, we are equally entitled to laugh at their author. This latter condition, however, is not indispensable, since the saying or expression has a comic virtue of its own. This is proved by the fact that we find it very difficult, in the majority of these cases, to say whom we are laughing at, although at times we have a dim, vague feeling that there is some one in the background.

Moreover, the person implicated is not always the speaker. Here it seems as though we should draw an important distinction between the *Witty (spirituel) and the Comic.* A word is said to be comic when it makes us laugh at the person who utters it, and witty when it makes us laugh either at a third party or at ourselves. But in most cases we can hardly make up our minds whether the word is comic or witty. All that we can say is that it is laughable.

Before proceeding, it might be well to examine more closely what is meant by ESPRIT. A witty saying makes us at least smile; consequently, no investigation into laughter would be complete did it not get to the bottom of the nature of wit and throw light on the underlying idea. It is to be feared, however, that this extremely subtle essence is one that evaporates when exposed to the light.

Let us first make a distinction between the two meanings of the word wit *esprit,* the broader one and the more restricted. In the broader meaning of the word, it would seem that what is called wit is a certain *dramatic* way of thinking. Instead of treating his ideas as mere symbols, the wit sees them, he hears them and, above all, makes them converse with one another like persons. He puts them on the stage, and himself, to some extent, into the bargain. A witty nation is, of necessity, a nation enamoured of the theatre. In every wit there is something of a poet – just as in every good reader there is the making of an actor. This comparison is made purposely, because a proportion might easily be established between the four terms. In order to read well we need only the intellectual side of the actor's art; but in order to act well one must be an actor in all one's soul and body. In just the same way, poetic creation calls for some degree of self-forgetfulness, whilst the wit does not usually err in this respect. We always get a glimpse of the latter behind what he says and does. He is not wholly engrossed in the business, because he only brings his intelligence into play. So any poet may reveal himself as a wit when he pleases. To do this there will be no need for him to acquire anything; it seems rather as though he would have to give up something. He would simply have to let his ideas hold converse with one another "for nothing, for the mere joy of the thing!" [9] He would only have to unfasten the double bond which keeps his ideas in touch with his feelings and his soul in touch with life. In short, he would turn into a wit by simply resolving to be no longer a poet in feeling, but only in intelligence.

But if wit consists, for the most part, in seeing things *sub specie theatri*, it is evidently capable of being specially directed to one variety of dramatic art, namely, comedy. Here we have a more restricted meaning of the term, and, moreover, the only one that interests us from the point of view of the theory of laughter. What is here called WIT is a gift for dashing off comic scenes in a few strokes – dashing them off, however, so subtly, delicately and rapidly, that all is over as soon as we begin to notice them.

Who are the actors in these scenes? With whom has the wit to deal? First of all, with his interlocutors themselves, when his witticism is a direct retort to one of them. Often with an absent person whom he supposes to have spoken and to whom he is replying. Still oftener, with the whole world, – in the ordinary meaning of the term, – which he takes to task, twisting a current idea into a paradox, or making use of a hackneyed phrase, or parodying some quotation or proverb. If we compare these scenes in miniature with one another, we find they are almost always variations of a comic theme with which we are well acquainted, that of the "robber robbed." You take up a metaphor, a phrase, an argument, and turn it against the man who is, or might be, its author, so that he is made to say what he did not mean to say and lets himself be caught, to some extent, in the toils of language. But the theme of the "robber robbed" is not the only possible one. We have gone over many varieties of the comic, and there is not one of them that is incapable of being volatilised into a witticism.

Every witty remark, then, lends itself to an analysis, whose chemical formula, so to say, we are now in a position to state. It runs as fol-

9 "Pour rien, pour le plaisir" is a quotation from Victor Hugo's Marion Delorme

lows: Take the remark, first enlarge it into a regular scene, then find out the category of the comic to which the scene evidently belongs: by this means you reduce the witty remark to its simplest elements and obtain a full explanation of it.

Let us apply this method to a classic example. "Your chest hurts me" (*j'ai mal a votre poitrine*) wrote Mme. de Sevigne to her ailing daughter – clearly a witty saying. If our theory is correct, we need only lay stress upon the saying, enlarge and magnify it, and we shall see it expand into a comic scene. Now, we find this very scene, ready made, in the AMOUR MEDECIN of Moliere. The sham doctor, Clitandre, who has been summoned to attend Sganarelle's daughter, contents himself with feeling Sganarelle's own pulse, whereupon, relying on the sympathy there must be between father and daughter, he unhesitatingly concludes: "Your daughter is very ill!" Here we have the transition from the witty to the comical. To complete our analysis, then, all we have to do is to discover what there is comical in the idea of giving a diagnosis of the child after sounding the father or the mother. Well, we know that one essential form of comic fancy lies in picturing to ourselves a living person as a kind of jointed dancing-doll, and that frequently, with the object of inducing us to form this mental picture, we are shown two or more persons speaking and acting as though attached to one another by invisible strings. Is not this the idea here suggested when we are led to materialise, so to speak, the sympathy we postulate as existing between father and daughter?

We now see how it is that writers on wit have perforce confined themselves to commenting on the extraordinary complexity of the things denoted by the term without ever succeeding in defining it. There are many ways of being witty, almost as many as there are of being the reverse. How can we detect what they have in common with one another, unless we first determine the general relationship between the witty and the comic? Once, however, this relationship is cleared up, everything is plain sailing. We then find the same connection between the comic and the witty as exists between a regular scene and the fugitive suggestion of a possible one. Hence, however numerous the forms assumed by the comic, wit will possess an equal number of corresponding varieties. So that the comic, in all its forms, is what should be defined first, by discovering (a task which is already quite difficult enough) the clue that leads from one form to the other. By that very operation wit will have been analysed, and will then appear as nothing more than the comic in a highly volatile state. To follow the opposite plan, however, and attempt directly to evolve a formula for wit, would be courting certain failure. What should we think of a chemist who, having ever so many jars of a certain substance in his laboratory, would prefer getting that substance from the atmosphere, in which merely infinitesimal traces of its vapour are to be found?

But this comparison between the witty and the comic is also indicative of the line we must take in studying the comic in words. On the one hand, indeed, we find there is no essential difference between a word that is comic and one that is witty; on the other hand, the latter, although connected with a figure of speech, invariably calls up the image, dim or distinct, of a comic scene. This amounts to saying that the comic in speech should correspond, point by point, with the comic in actions and in situations, and is nothing more, if one may so express oneself, than their projection on to the plane of words. So let us return to the comic in actions and in situations, consider the chief methods by which it is obtained, and apply them to the choice of words and the building up of sentences. We shall thus have every possible form of the comic in words as well as every variety of wit.

i.　　Inadvertently to say or do what we have no intention of saying or doing, as a result of inelasticity or momentum, is, as we are aware, one of the main sources of the comic. Thus, absentmindedness is essentially laughable, and so we laugh at anything rigid, readymade, mechanical in gesture, attitude and even facial expression. Do we find this kind of rigidity in language also? No doubt we do, since language contains ready-made formulas and stereotyped phrases. The man who always expressed himself in such terms would invariably be comic. But if an isolated phrase is to be comic in itself, when once separated from the person who utters it, it must be something more than ready-made, it must bear within itself some sign which tells us, beyond the possibility of doubt, that it was uttered automatically. This can only happen when the phrase embodies some evident absurdity, either a palpable error or a contradiction in terms. Hence the following general rule: *A comic meaning is invariably obtained when an absurd idea is fitted into a well-established phrase-form.*

"Ce sabre est le plus beau jour de ma vie," said M. Prudhomme. Translate the phrase into English or German and it becomes purely absurd, though it is comic enough in French. The reason is that "le plus beau jour de ma vie" is one of those ready-made phrase-endings to which a Frenchman's ear is accustomed. To make it comic, then, we need only clearly indicate the automatism of the person who utters it. This is what we get when we introduce an absurdity into the phrase. Here the absurdity is by no means the source of the comic, it is only a very simple and effective means of making it obvious.

We have quoted only one saying of M. Prudhomme, but the majority of those attributed to him belong to the same class. M. Prudhomme is a man of ready-made phrases. And as there are ready-made phrases in all languages, M. Prudhomme is always capable of being transposed, though seldom of being translated. At times the commonplace phrase, under cover of which the absurdity slips in, is not so readily noticeable. "I don't like working between meals," said a lazy lout. There would be nothing amusing in the saying did there not exist that salutary precept in the realm of hygiene: "One should not eat between meals."

Sometimes, too, the effect is a complicated one. Instead of one commonplace phrase-form, there are two or three which are dovetailed into each other. Take, for instance, the remark of one of the characters in a play by Labiche, "Only God has the right to kill His fellow-creature." It would seem that advantage is here taken of two separate familiar sayings; "It is God who disposes of the lives of men," and, "It is criminal for a man to kill his fellow-creature." But the two sayings are combined so as to deceive the ear and leave the impression of being one of those hackneyed sentences that are accepted as a matter of course. Hence our attention nods, until we are suddenly aroused by the absurdity of the meaning. These examples suffice to show how one of the most important types of the comic can be projected – in a simplified form – on the plane of speech. We will now proceed to a form which is not so general.

2.   "We laugh if our attention is diverted to the physical in a person when it is the moral that is in question," is a law we laid down in the first part of this work. Let us apply it to language. Most words might be said to have a *physical* and a *moral* meaning, according as they are interpreted literally or figuratively. Every word, indeed, begins by denoting a concrete object or a material action; but by degrees the meaning of the word is refined into an abstract relation or a pure idea. If, then, the above law holds good here, it should be stated as follows: "A comic effect is obtained whenever we pretend to take literally an expression which was used figuratively"; or, "Once our attention is fixed on the material aspect of a metaphor, the idea expressed becomes comic."

In the phrase, "Tous les arts sont freres" (all the arts are brothers), the word "frere" (brother) is used metaphorically to indicate a more or less striking resemblance. The word is so often used in this way, that when we hear it we do not think of the concrete, the material connection implied in every relationship. We should notice it more if we were told that "Tous les arts sont cousins," for the word "cousin" is not so often employed in a figurative sense; that is why the word here already assumes a slight tinge of the comic. But let us go further still, and suppose that our attention is attracted to the material side of the metaphor by the choice of a relationship which is incompatible with the gender of the two words composing the metaphorical expression: we get a laughable result. Such is the well-known saying, also attributed to M. Prudhomme, "Tous les arts (masculine) sont soeurs (feminine)." "He is always running after a joke," was said in Boufflers' presence regarding a very conceited fellow. Had Boufflers replied, "He won't catch it," that would have been the beginning of a witty saying, though nothing more than the beginning, for the word "catch" is interpreted figuratively almost as often as the word "run"; nor does it compel us more strongly than the latter to materialise the image of two runners, the one at the heels of the other. In order that the rejoinder may appear to be a thoroughly witty one, we must borrow from the language of sport an expression so vivid and concrete that we cannot refrain from witnessing the race in good earnest. This is what Boufflers does when he retorts, "I'll back the joke!"

We said that wit often consists in extending the idea of one's interlocutor to the point of making him express the opposite of what he thinks and getting him, so to say, entrapt by his own words. We must now add that this trap is almost always some metaphor or comparison the concrete aspect of which is turned against him. You may remember the dialogue between a mother and her son in the Faux Bonshommes: "My dear boy, gambling on 'Change is very risky. You win one day and lose the next." – "Well, then, I will gamble only every other day." In the same play too we find the following edifying conversation between two company-promoters: "Is this a very honourable thing we are doing? These unfortunate shareholders, you see, we are taking the money out of their very pockets...." – "Well, out of what do you expect us to take it?"

An amusing result is likewise obtainable whenever a symbol or an emblem is expanded on its concrete side, and a pretence is made of retaining the same symbolical value for this expansion as for the emblem itself. In a very lively comedy we are introduced to a Monte Carlo official, whose uniform is covered with medals, although he has only received a single decoration. "You see, I staked my medal on a number at roulette," he said, "and as the number turned up, I was entitled to thirty-six times my stake." This reasoning is very similar to that offered by Giboyer in the Effrontes. Criticism is made of a bride of forty summers who is wearing orange-blossoms with her wedding costume: "Why, she was entitled to oranges, let alone orange-blossoms!" remarked Giboyer.

But we should never cease were we to take one by one all the laws we have stated, and try to prove them on what we have called the plane of language. We had better confine ourselves to the three general propositions of the preceding section. We have shown that "series of events" may become comic either by repetition, by inversion, or by reciprocal interference. Now we shall see that this is also the case with series of words.

To take series of events and repeat them in another key or another environment, or to invert them whilst still leaving them a certain meaning, or mix them up so that their respective meanings jostle one another, is invariably comic, as we have already said, for it is getting life to submit to be treated as a machine. But thought, too, is a living thing. And language, the translation of thought, should be just as living. We may thus surmise that a phrase is likely to become comic if, though reversed, it still makes sense, or if it expresses equally well two quite independent sets of ideas, or, finally, if it has been obtained by transposing an idea into some key other than its own. Such, indeed, are the three fundamental laws of what might be called *the comic transformation of sentences,* as we shall show by a few examples.

Let it first be said that these three laws are far from being of equal importance as regards the theory of the ludicrous. *inversion* is the least interesting of the three. It must be easy of application, however, for it is noticeable that, no sooner do professional wits hear a sentence spoken than they experiment to see if a meaning cannot be obtained by reversing it, – by putting, for instance, the subject in place of the object, and the object in place of the subject. It is not unusual for this device to be employed for refuting an idea in more or less humorous terms. One of the characters in a comedy of Labiche shouts out to his neighbour on the floor above, who is in the habit of dirtying his balcony, "What do you mean by emptying your pipe on to my terrace?" The neighbour retorts, "What do you mean by putting your terrace under my pipe?" There is no necessity to dwell upon this kind of wit, instances of which could easily be multiplied. The *Reciprocal Interference* of two sets of ideas in the same sentence is an inexhaustible source of amusing varieties. There are many ways of bringing about this interference, I mean of bracketing in the same expression two independent meanings that apparently tally. The least reputable of these ways is the pun. In the pun, the same sentence appears to offer two independent meanings, but it is only an appearance; in reality there are two different sentences made up of different words, but claiming to be one and the same because both have the same sound. We pass from the pun, by imperceptible stages, to the true play upon words. Here there is really one and the same sentence through which two different sets of ideas are expressed, and we are confronted with only one series of words; but advantage is taken of the different meanings a word may have, especially when used figuratively instead of literally. So that in fact there is often only a slight difference between the play upon words on the one hand, and a poetic metaphor or an illuminating comparison on the other. Whereas an illuminating comparison and a striking image always seem to reveal the close harmony that exists between language and nature, regarded as two parallel forms of life, the play upon words makes us think somehow of a negligence on the part of language, which, for the time being, seems to have forgotten its real function and now claims to accommodate things to itself instead of accommodating itself to things. And so the play upon words always betrays a momentary *lapse of attention* in language, and it is precisely on that account that it is amusing.

Inversion and Reciprocal Interference, after all, are only a certain playfulness of the mind which ends at playing upon words. The comic in *transposition* is much more far-reaching. Indeed, transposition is to ordinary language what repetition is to comedy.

We said that repetition is the favourite method of classic comedy. It consists in so arranging events that a scene is reproduced either between the same characters under fresh circumstances or between fresh characters under the same circumstances. Thus we have, repeated by lackeys in less dignified language, a scene already played by their masters. Now, imagine ideas expressed in suitable style and thus placed in the setting of their natural environment. If you think of some arrangement whereby they are transferred to fresh surroundings, while maintaining their mutual relations, or, in other words, if you can induce them to express themselves in an altogether different style and to transpose themselves into another key, you will have language itself playing a comedy – language itself made comic. There will be no need, moreover, actually to set before us both expressions of the same ideas, the transposed expression and the natural one. For we are acquainted with the natural one – the one which we should have chosen instinctively. So it will be enough if the effort of comic invention bears on the other, and on the other alone. No sooner is the second set before us than we spontaneously supply the first. Hence the following general rule: *A comic effect is always obtainable by transposing the nature expression of an idea into another key.*

The means of transposition are so many and varied, language affords so rich a continuity of themes and the comic is here capable of passing through so great a number of stages, from the most insipid buffoonery up to the loftiest forms of humour and irony, that we shall forego the attempt to make out a complete list. Having stated the rule, we will simply, here and there, verify its main applications.

In the first place, we may distinguish two keys at the extreme ends of the scale, the solemn and the familiar. The most obvious effects are obtained by merely transposing the one into the other, which thus provides us with two opposite currents of comic fancy.

Transpose the solemn into the familiar and the result is parody. The effect of parody, thus defined, extends to instances in which the idea expressed in familiar terms is one that, if only in deference to custom, ought to be pitched in another key. Take as an example the following description of the dawn, quoted by Jean Paul Richter: "The sky was beginning to change from black to red, like a lobster being boiled." Note that the expression of old-world matters in terms of modern life produces the same effect, by reason of the halo of poetry which surrounds classical antiquity.

It is doubtless the comic in parody that has suggested to some philosophers, and in particular to Alexander Bain, the idea of defining the comic, in general, as a species of *degradation*. They describe the laughable as causing something to appear mean that was formerly dignified. But if our analysis is correct, degradation is only one form of transposition, and transposition itself only one of the means of obtaining laughter. There is a host of others, and the source of laughter must be sought for much further back. Moreover, without going so far, we see that while the transposition from solemn to trivial, from better to worse, is comic, the inverse transposition may be even more so.

It is met with as often as the other, and, apparently, we may distinguish two main forms of it, according as it refers to the *physical dimensions* of an object or to its *moral value*.

To speak of small things as though they were large is, in a general way, *to exaggerate*. Exaggeration is always comic when prolonged, and especially when systematic; then, indeed, it appears as one method of transposition. It excites so much laughter that some writers have been led to define the comic as exaggeration, just as others have defined it as degradation. As a matter of fact, exaggeration, like degradation, is only one form of one kind of the comic. Still, it is a very striking form. It has given birth to the mock-heroic poem, a rather old-fashioned device, I admit, though traces of it are still to be found in persons inclined to exaggerate methodically. It might often be said of braggadocio that it is its mock-heroic aspect which makes us laugh.

Far more artificial, but also far more refined, is the transposition upwards from below when applied to the moral value of things, not to their physical dimensions. To express in reputable language some disreputable idea, to take some scandalous situation, some low-class calling or disgraceful behaviour, and describe them in terms of the utmost *"Respectability,"* is generally comic. The English word is here purposely employed, as the practice itself is characteristically English. Many instances of it may be found in Dickens and Thackeray, and in English literature generally. Let us remark, in passing, that the intensity of the effect does not here depend on its length. A word is sometimes sufficient, provided it gives us a glimpse of an entire system of transposition accepted in certain social circles and reveals, as it were, a moral organisation of immorality. Take the following remark made by an official to one of his subordinates in a novel of Gogol's, "Your peculations are too extensive for an official of your rank."

Summing up the foregoing, then, there are two extreme terms of comparison, the very large and the very small, the best and the worst, between which transposition may be effected in one direction or the other. Now, if the interval be gradually narrowed, the contrast between the terms obtained will be less and less violent, and the varieties of comic transposition more and more subtle.

The most common of these contrasts is perhaps that between the real and the ideal, between what is and what ought to be. Here again transposition may take place in either direction. Sometimes we state what ought to be done, and pretend to believe that this is just what is actually being done; then we have *irony*. Sometimes, on the contrary, we describe with scrupulous minuteness what is being done, and pretend to believe that this is just what ought to be done; such is often the method of *humour*. Humour, thus denned, is the counterpart of irony. Both are forms of satire, but irony is oratorical in its nature, whilst humour partakes of the scientific. Irony is emphasised the higher we allow ourselves to be uplifted by the idea of the good that ought to be: thus irony may grow so hot within us that it becomes a kind of high-pressure eloquence. On the other hand, humour is the more emphasised the deeper we go down into an evil that actually is, in order t o set down its details in the most cold-blooded indifference. Several authors, Jean Paul amongst them, have noticed that humour delights in concrete terms, technical details, definite facts. If our analysis is correct, this is not an accidental trait of humour, it is its very essence. A humorist is a moralist disguised as a scientist, something like an anatomist who practises dissection with the sole object of filling us with disgust; so that humour, in the restricted sense in which we are here regarding the word, is really a transposition from the moral to the scientific.

By still further curtailing the interval between the terms transposed, we may now obtain more and more specialised types of comic transpositions. Thus, certain professions have a technical vocabulary: what a wealth of laughable results have been obtained by transposing the ideas of everyday life into this professional jargon! Equally comic is the extension of business phraseology to the social relations of life, – for instance, the phrase of one of Labiche's characters in allusion to an invitation he has received, "Your kindness of the third ult.," thus transposing the commercial formula, "Your favour of the third instant." This class of the comic, moreover, may attain a special profundity of its own when it discloses not merely a professional practice, but a fault in character. Recall to mind the scenes in the Faux Bonshommes and the Famille Benoiton, where marriage is dealt with as a business affair, and matters of sentiment are set down in strictly commercial language.

Here, however, we reach the point at which peculiarities of language really express peculiarities of character, a closer investigation of which we must hold over to the next chapter. Thus, as might have been expected and may be seen from the foregoing, the comic in words follows closely on the comic in situation and is finally merged, along with the latter, in the comic in character. Language only attains laughable results because it is a human product, modelled as exactly as possible on the forms of the human mind. We feel it contains some living element of our own life; and if this life of language were complete and perfect, if there were nothing stereotype in it, if, in short, language were an absolutely unified organism incapable of being split up into independent organisms, it would evade the comic as would a soul whose life was one harmonious whole, unruffled as the calm surface of a peaceful lake.

There is no pool, however, which has not some dead leaves floating on its surface, no human soul upon which there do not settle habits that make it rigid against itself by making it rigid against others, no language, in short, so subtle and instinct with life, so fully alert in each of its parts as to eliminate the ready-made and oppose the mechanical operations of inversion, transposition, etc., which one would fain perform upon it as on some lifeless thing. The rigid, the ready – made, the mechanical, in contrast with the supple, the ever-changing and the living, absentmindedness in contrast with attention, in a word, automatism in contrast with free activity, such are the defects that laughter singles out and would fain correct. We appealed to this idea to give us light at the outset, when starting upon the analysis of the ludicrous. We have seen it shining at every decisive turning in our road. With its help, we shall now enter upon a more important investigation, one that will, we hope, be more instructive. We purpose, in short, studying comic characters, or rather determining the essential conditions of comedy in character, while endeavouring to bring it about that this study may contribute to a better understanding of the real nature of art and the general relation between art and life.

CHAPTER III

THE COMIC IN CHARACTER

I

We have followed the comic along many of its winding channels in an endeavour to discover how it percolates into a form, an attitude, or a gesture; a situation, an action, or an expression. The analysis of comic *characters* has now brought us to the most important part of our task. It would also be the most difficult, had we yielded to the temptation of defining the laughable by a few striking – and consequently obvious – examples; for then, in proportion as we advanced towards the loftiest manifestations of the comic, we should have found the facts slipping between the over-wide meshes of the definition intended to retain them. But, as a matter of fact, we have followed the opposite plan, by throwing light on the subject from above. Convinced that laughter has a social meaning and import, that the comic expresses, above all else, a special lack of adaptability to society, and that, in short, there is nothing comic apart from man, we have made man and character generally our main objective. Our chief difficulty, therefore, has lain in explaining how we come to laugh at anything else than character, and by what subtle processes of fertilisation, combination or amalgamation, the comic can worm its way into a mere movement, an impersonal situation, or an independent phrase. This is what we have done so far. We started with the pure metal, and all our endeavours have been directed solely towards reconstructing the ore. It is the metal itself we are now about to study. Nothing could be easier, for this time we have a simple element to deal with. Let us examine it closely and see how it reacts upon everything else.

There are moods, we said, which move us as soon us as soon as we perceive them, joys and sorrows with which we sympathise, passions and vices which call forth painful astonishment, terror or pity, in the beholder; in short, sentiments that are prolonged in sentimental overtones from mind to mind. All this concerns the essentials of life. All this is serious, at times even tragic. Comedy can only begin at the point where our neighbour's personality ceases to affect us. It begins, in fact, with what might be called a growing callousness to social life. Any individual is comic who automatically goes his own way without troubling himself about getting into touch with the rest of his fellow-beings. It is the part of laughter to reprove his absentmindedness and wake him out of his dream. If it is permissible to compare important things with trivial ones, we would call to mind what happens when a youth enters one of our military academies. After getting through the dreaded ordeal of the examination, he finds the has other ordeals to face, which his seniors have arranged with the object of fitting him for the new life he is entering upon, or, as they say, of "breaking him into harness." Every small society that forms within the larger is thus impelled, by a vague kind of instinct, to devise some method of discipline or "breaking in," so as to deal with the rigidity of habits that have been formed elsewhere and have now to undergo a partial modification. Society, properly so-called, proceeds in exactly the same way. Each member must be ever attentive to his social surroundings; he must model himself on his environment; in short, he must avoid shutting himself up in his own peculiar character as a philosopher in his ivory tower. Therefore society holds suspended over each individual member, if not the threat of correction, at all events the prospect of a snubbing, which, although it is slight, is none the less dreaded. Such must be the function of laughter. Always rather humiliating for the one against whom it is directed, laughter is, really and truly, a kind of social "ragging."

Hence the equivocal nature of the comic. It belongs neither altogether to art nor altogether to life. On the one hand, characters in real life would never make us laugh were we not capable of watching their vagaries in the same way as we look down at a play from our seat in a box; they are only comic in our eyes because they perform a kind of comedy before us. But, on the other hand, the pleasure caused by laughter, even on the stage, is not an unadulterated enjoyment; it is not a pleasure that is exclusively esthetic or altogether disinterested. It always implies a secret or unconscious intent, if not of each one of us, at all events of society as a whole. In laughter we always find an unavowed intention to humiliate, and consequently to correct our neighbour, if not in his will, at least in his deed. This is the reason a comedy is far more like real life than a drama is. The more sublime the drama, the more profound the analysis to which the poet has had to subject the raw materials of daily life in order to obtain the tragic element in its unadulterated form. On the contrary, it is only in its lower aspects, in light comedy and farce, that comedy is in striking contrast to reality: the higher it rises, the more it approximates to life; in fact, there are scenes in real life so closely bordering on high-class comedy that the stage might adopt them without changing a single word.

Hence it follows that the elements of comic character on the stage and in actual life will be the same. What are these elements? We shall find no difficulty in deducing them. It has often been said that it is the *trifling* faults of our fellow-men that make us laugh.

Evidently there is a considerable amount of truth in this opinion; still, it cannot be regarded as altogether correct. First, as regards faults, it is no easy matter to draw the line between the trifling and the serious; maybe it is not because a fault is trifling that it makes us laugh, but rather because it makes us laugh that we regard it as trifling, for there is nothing disarms us like laughter. But we may go even farther, and maintain that there are faults at which we laugh, even though fully aware that they are serious, – Harpagon's avarice, for instance. And then, we may as well confess – though somewhat reluctantly – that we laugh not only at the faults of our fellow-men, but also, at times, at their good qualities. We laugh at Alceste. The objection may be urged that it is not the earnestness of Alceste that is ludicrous, but rather the special aspect which earnestness assumes in his case, and, in short, a certain eccentricity that mars it in our eyes. Agreed; but it is none the less true that this eccentricity in Alceste, at which we laugh, *makes his earnestness laughable,* and that is the main point. So we may conclude that the ludicrous is not always an indication of a fault, in the moral meaning of the word, and if critics insist on seeing a fault, even though a trifling one, in the ludicrous, they must point out what it is here that exactly distinguishes the trifling from the serious.

The truth is, the comic character may, strictly speaking, be quite in accord with stern morality. All it has to do is to bring itself into accord with society. The character of Alceste is that of a thoroughly honest man. But then he is unsociable, and, on that very account, ludicrous. A flexible vice may not be so easy to ridicule as a rigid virtue. It is rigidity that society eyes with suspicion. Consequently, it is the rigidity of Alceste that makes us laugh, though here rigidity stands for honesty. The man who withdraws into himself is liable to ridicule, because the comic is largely made up of this very withdrawal. This accounts for the comic being so frequently dependent on the manners or ideas, or, to put it bluntly, on the prejudices, of a society.

It must be acknowledged, however, to the credit of mankind, that there is no essential difference between the social ideal and the rule, that it is the faults of others that make us laugh, provided we add that they make us laugh by reason of their *unsociability* rather than of their *immorality*. What, then, are the faults capable of becoming ludicrous, and in what circumstances do we regard them as being too serious to be laughed at?

We have already given an implicit answer to this question. The comic, we said, appeals to the intelligence, pure and simple; laughter is incompatible with emotion. Depict some fault, however trifling, in such a way as to arouse sympathy, fear, or pity; the mischief is done, it is impossible for us to laugh. On the other hand, take a downright vice, – even one that is, generally speaking, of an odious nature, – you may make it ludicrous if, by some suitable contrivance, you arrange so that it leaves our emotions unaffected. Not that the vice must then be ludicrous, but it MAY, from that time forth, become so. IT MUST NOT AROUSE OUR FEELINGS; that is the sole condition really necessary, though assuredly it is not sufficient.

But, then, how will the comic poet set to work to prevent our feelings being moved? The question is an embarrassing one. To clear it up thoroughly, we should have to enter upon a rather novel line of investigation, to analyse the artificial sympathy which we bring with us to the theatre, and determine upon the circumstances in which we accept and those in which we refuse to share imaginary joys and sorrows. There is an art of lulling sensibility to sleep and providing it with dreams, as happens in the case of a mesmerised person. And there is also an art of throwing a wet blanket upon sympathy at the very moment it might arise, the result being that the situation, though a serious one, is not taken seriously. This latter art would appear to be governed by two methods, which are applied more or less unconsciously by the comic poet. The first consists in *isolating*, within the soul of the character, the feeling attributed to him, and making it a parasitic organism, so to speak, endowed with an independent existence. As a general rule, an intense feeling successively encroaches upon all other mental states and colours them with its own peculiar hue; if, then, we are made to witness this gradual impregnation, we finally become impregnated ourselves with a corresponding emotion. To employ a different image, an emotion may be said to be dramatic and contagious when all the harmonics in it are heard along with the fundamental note. It is because the actor thus thrills throughout his whole being that the spectators themselves feel the thrill. On the contrary, in the case of emotion that leaves us indifferent and that is about to become comic, there is always present a certain rigidity which prevents it from establishing a connection with the rest of the soul in which it has taken up its abode. This rigidity may be manifested, when the time comes, by puppet-like movements, and then it will provoke laughter; but, before that, it had already alienated our sympathy: how can we put ourselves in tune with a soul which is not in tune with itself? In Moliere's L'Avare we have a scene bordering upon drama. It is the one in which the borrower and the usurer, who have never seen each other, meet face to face and find that they are son and father. Here we should be in the thick of a drama, if only greed and fatherly affection, conflicting with each other in the soul of Harpagon, had effected a more or less original combination. But such is not the case. No sooner has the interview come to an end than the father forgets everything. On meeting his son again he barely alludes to the scene, serious though it has been: "You, my son, whom I am good enough to forgive your recent escapade, etc." Greed has thus passed close to all other feelings *absentmindedly*, without either touching them or being touched. Although it has taken up its abode in the soul and become master of the house, none the less it remains a stranger. Far different would be avarice of a tragic sort. We should find it attracting and absorbing, transforming and assimilating the divers energies of the man: feelings and affections, likes and dislikes, vices and virtues, would all become something into which avarice would breathe a new kind of life. Such seems to be the first essential difference between high-class comedy and drama.

There is a second, which is far more obvious and arises out of the first. When a mental state is depicted to us with the object of making it dramatic, or even merely of inducing us to take it seriously, it gradually crystallises into *actions* which provide the real measure of its greatness. Thus, the miser orders his whole life with a view to acquiring wealth, and the pious hypocrite, though pretending to have his eyes fixed upon heaven, steers most skilfully his course here below. Most certainly, comedy does not shut out calculations of this kind; we need only take as an example the very machinations of Tartuffe. But that is what comedy has in common with drama; and in order to keep distinct from it, to prevent our taking a serious action seriously, in short, in order to prepare us for laughter, comedy utilises a method, the formula of which may be given as follows: *Instead of concentrating our attention on actions, comedy directs it rather to gestures.* By *gestures* we here mean the attitudes, the movements and even the language by which a mental state expresses itself outwardly without any aim or profit, from no other cause than a kind of inner itching. Gesture, thus defined, is profoundly different from action. Action is intentional or, at any rate, conscious; gesture slips out unawares, it is automatic. In action, the entire person is engaged; in gesture, an isolated part of the person is expressed, unknown to, or at least apart from, the whole of the personality. Lastly – and here is the essential point – action is in exact proportion to the feeling that inspires it: the one gradually passes into the other, so that we may allow our sympathy or our aversion to glide along the line running from feeling to action and become increasingly interested. About gesture, however, there is something explosive, which awakes our sensibility when on the point of being lulled to sleep and, by thus rousing us up, prevents our taking matters seriously. Thus, as soon as our attention is fixed on gesture and not on action, we are in the realm of comedy. Did we merely take his actions into account, Tartuffe would belong to drama: it is only when we take his gestures into consideration that we find him comic. You may remember how he comes on to the stage with the words: "Laurent, lock up my hair-shirt and my scourge." He knows Dorine is listening to him, but doubtless he would say the same if she were not there. He enters so thoroughly into the role of a hypocrite that he plays it almost sincerely. In this way, and this way only, can he become comic. Were it not for this material sincerity, were it not for the language and attitudes that his long-standing experience as a hypocrite has transformed into natural gestures, Tartuffe would be simply odious, because we should only think of what is meant and willed in his conduct. And so we see why action is essential in drama, but only accessory in comedy. In a comedy, we feel any other situation might equally well have been chosen for the purpose of introducing the character; he would still have been the same man though the situation were different. But we do not get this impression in a drama. Here characters and situations are welded together, or rather, events form part and parcel with the persons, so that were the drama to tell us a different story, even though the actors kept the same names, we should in reality be dealing with other persons.

To sum up, whether a character is good or bad is of little moment: granted he is unsociable, he is capable of becoming comic. We now see that the seriousness of the case is of no importance either: whether serious or trifling, it is still capable of making us laugh, provided that care be taken not to arouse our emotions. Unsociability in the performer and insensibility in the spectator – such, in a word, are the two essential conditions. There is a third, implicit in the other two, which so far it has been the aim of our analysis to bring out.

This third condition is automatism. We have pointed it out from the outset of this work, continually drawing attention to the following point: what is essentially laughable is what is done automatically. In a vice, even in a virtue, the comic is that element by which the person unwittingly betrays himself – the involuntary gesture or the unconscious remark. Absentmindedness is always comical. Indeed, the deeper the absentmindedness the higher the comedy. Systematic absentmindedness, like that of Don Quixote, is the most comical thing imaginable: it is the comic itself, drawn as nearly as possible from its very source. Take any other comic character: however unconscious he may be of what he says or does, he cannot be comical unless there be some aspect of his person of which he is unaware, one side of his nature which he overlooks; on that account alone does he make us laugh.[10] Profoundly comic sayings are those artless ones in which some vice reveals itself in all its nakedness: how could it thus expose itself were it capable of seeing itself as it is? It is not uncommon for a comic character to condemn in general terms a certain line of conduct and immediately afterwards afford an example of it himself: for instance, M. Jourdain's teacher of philosophy flying into a passion after inveighing against anger; Vadius taking a poem from his pocket after heaping ridicule on readers of poetry, etc. What is the object of such contradictions except to help us to put our finger on the obliviousness of the characters to their own actions? Inattention to self, and consequently to others, is what we invariably find. And if we look at the matter closely, we see that inattention is here equivalent to what we have called unsociability. The chief cause of rigidity is the neglect to look around – and more especially within oneself: how can a man fashion his personality after that of another if he does not first study others as well as himself? Rigidity, automatism, absent-mindedness and unsociability are all inextricably entwined; and all serve as ingredients to the making up of the comic in character.

In a word, if we leave on one side, when dealing with human personality, that portion which interests our sensibility or appeals to our feeling, all the rest is capable of becoming comic, and the comic will be

---

10 When the humorist laughs at himself, he is really acting a double part; the self who laughs is indeed conscious, but not the self who is laughed at.

proportioned to the rigidity. We formulated this idea at the outset of this work. We have verified it in its main results, and have just applied it to the definition of comedy. Now we must get to closer quarters, and show how it enables us to delimitate the exact position comedy occupies among all the other arts. In one sense it might be said that all character is comic, provided we mean by character the ready-made element in our personality, that mechanical element which resembles a piece of clock-work wound up once for all and capable of working automatically. It is, if you will, that which causes us to imitate ourselves. And it is also, for that very reason, that which enables others to imitate us. Every comic character is a type. Inversely, every resemblance to a type has something comic in it. Though we may long have associated with an individual without discovering anything about him to laugh at, still, if advantage is t taken of some accidental analogy to dub him with the name of a famous hero of romance or drama, he will in our eyes border upon the ridiculous, if only for a moment. And yet this hero of romance may not be a comic character at all. But then it is comic to be like him. It is comic to wander out of one's own self. It is comic to fall into a ready-made category. And what is most comic of all is to become a category oneself into which others will fall, as into a ready-made frame; it is to crystallise into a stock character.

Thus, to depict characters, that is to say, general types, is the object of high-class comedy. This has often been said. But it is as well to repeat it, since there could be no better definition of comedy. Not only are we entitled to say that comedy gives us general types, but we might add that it is the *only* one of all the arts that aims at the general; so that once this objective has been attributed to it, we have said all that it is and all that the rest cannot be. To prove that such is really the essence of comedy, and that it is in this respect opposed to tragedy, drama and the other forms of art, we should begin by defining art in its higher forms: then, gradually coming down to comic poetry, we should find that this latter is situated on the border-line between art and life, and that, by the generality of its subject-matter, it contrasts with the rest of the arts. We cannot here plunge into so vast a subject of investigation; but we needs must sketch its main outlines, lest we overlook what, to our mind, is essential on the comic stage.

What is the object of art? Could reality come into direct contact with sense and consciousness, could we enter into immediate communion with things and with ourselves, probably art would be useless, or rather we should all be artists, for then our soul would continually vibrate in perfect accord with nature. Our eyes, aided by memory, would carve out in space and fix in time the most inimitable of pictures. Hewn in the living marble of the human form, fragments of statues, beautiful as the relics of antique statuary, would strike the passing glance. Deep in our souls we should hear the strains of our inner life's unbroken melody, – a music that is ofttimes gay, but more frequently plaintive and always original. All this is around and within us, and yet no whit of it do we distinctly perceive. Between nature and ourselves, nay, between ourselves and our own consciousness a veil is interposed: a veil that is dense and opaque for the common herd, – thin, almost transparent, for the artist and the poet. What fairy wove that veil? Was it done in malice or in friendliness? We had to live, and life demands that we grasp things in their relations to our own needs. Life is action. Life implies the acceptance only of the *utilitarian* side of things in order to respond to them by appropriate reactions: all other impressions must be dimmed or else reach us vague and blurred. I look and I think I see, I listen and I think I hear, I examine myself and I think I am reading the very depths of my heart. But what I see and hear of the outer world is purely and simply a selection made by my senses to serve as a light to my conduct; what I know of myself is what comes to the surface, what participates in my actions. My senses and my consciousness, therefore, give me no more than a practical simplification of reality. In the vision they furnish me of myself and of things, the differences that are useless to man are obliterated, the resemblances that are useful to him are emphasised; ways are traced out for me in advance, along which my activity is to travel. These ways are the ways which all mankind has trod before me. Things have been classified with a view to the use I can derive from them. And it is this classification I perceive, far more clearly than the colour and the shape of things. Doubtless man is vastly superior to the lower animals in this respect. It is not very likely that the eye of a wolf makes any distinction between a kid and a lamb; both appear t o the wolf as the same identical quarry, alike easy to pounce upon, alike good to devour. We, for our part, make a distinction between a goat and a sheep; but can we tell one goat from another, one sheep from another? The *individuality* of things or of beings escapes us, unless it is materially to our advantage to perceive it. Even when we do take note of it – as when we distinguish one man from another – it is not the individuality itself that the eye grasps, i.e., an entirely original harmony of forms and colours, but only one or two features that will make practical recognition easier.

In short, we do not see the actual things themselves; in most cases we confine ourselves to reading the labels affixed to them. This tendency, the result of need, has become even more pronounced under the influence of speech; for words – with the exception of proper nouns – all denote genera. The word, which only takes note of the most ordinary function and commonplace aspect of the thing, intervenes between it and ourselves, and would conceal its form from our eyes, were that form not already masked beneath the necessities that brought the word into existence. Not only external objects, but even our own mental states, are screened from us in their inmost, their personal aspect, in the original life they possess. When we feel love or hatred, when we are gay or sad, is it really the feeling itself that reaches our consciousness with those innumerable fleeting shades of meaning and deep resounding echoes that make it something altogether our own? We should all, were it so, be novelists or poets or musicians. Mostly, however, we perceive nothing but the outward display of our mental state. We catch only the impersonal aspect of our feelings, that aspect which speech has set down once for all because it is almost the same, in the same conditions, for all men. Thus, even in our own individual, individuality escapes our ken. We move amidst generalities and symbols, as within a tilt-yard in which our force is effectively pitted against other forces; and fascinated by action, tempted by it, for our own good, on to the field it has selected, we live in a zone midway between things and ourselves, externally to things, externally also to ourselves. From time to time, however, in a fit of absentmindedness, nature raises up souls that are more detached from life. Not with that intentional, logical, systematical detachment – the result of reflection and philosophy – but rather with natural detachment, one innate in the structure of sense or consciousness, which at once reveals itself by a virginal manner, so to speak, of seeing, hearing or thinking. Were this detachment complete, did the soul no longer cleave to action by any of its perceptions, it would be the soul of an artist such as the world has never yet seen. It would excel alike in every art at the same time; or rather, it would fuse them all into one. It would perceive all things in their native purity: the forms, colours, sounds of the physical world as well as the subtlest movements of the inner life. But this is asking too much of nature. Even for such of us as she has made artists, it is by accident, and on one side only, that she has lifted the veil. In one direction only has she forgotten to rivet the perception to the need. And since each direction corresponds to what we call a SENSE – through one of his senses, and through that sense alone, is the artist usually wedded to art. Hence, originally, the diversity of arts. Hence also the speciality of predispositions. This one applies himself to colours and forms, and since he loves colour for colour and form for form, since he perceives them for their sake and not for his own, it is the inner life of things that he sees appearing through their forms and colours. Little by little he insinuates it into our own perception, baffled though we may be at the outset. For a few moments at least, he diverts us from the prejudices of form and colour that come between ourselves and reality. And thus he realises the loftiest ambition of art, which here consists in revealing to us nature. Others, again, retire within themselves. Beneath the thousand rudimentary actions which are the outward and visible signs of an emotion, behind the commonplace, conventional expression that both reveals and conceals an individual mental state, it is the emotion, the original mood, to which they attain in its undefiled essence. And then, to induce us to make the same effort ourselves, they contrive to make us see something of what they have seen: by rhythmical arrangement of words, which thus become organised and animated with a life of their own, they tell us – or rather suggest – things that speech was not calculated to express. Others delve yet deeper still. Beneath these joys and sorrows which can, at a pinch, be translated into language, they grasp something that has nothing in common with language, certain rhythms of life and breath that. are closer to man than his inmost feelings, being the living law – varying with each individual – of his enthusiasm and despair, his hopes and regrets. By setting free and emphasising this music, they force it upon our attention; they compel us, willy-nilly, to fall in with it, like passers-by who join in a dance. And thus they impel us to set in motion, in the depths of our being, some secret chord which was only waiting to thrill. So art, whether it be painting or sculpture, poetry or music, has no other object than to brush aside the utilitarian symbols, the conventional and socially accepted generalities, in short, everything that veils reality from us, in order to bring us face to face with reality itself. It is from a misunderstanding on this point that the dispute between realism and idealism in art has arisen. Art is certainly only a more direct vision of reality. But this purity of perception implies a break with utilitarian convention, an innate and specially localised disinterestedness of sense or consciousness, in short, a certain immateriality of life, which is what has always been called idealism. So that we might say, without in any way playing upon the meaning of the words, that realism is in the work when idealism is in the soul, and that it is only through ideality that we can resume contact with reality.

Dramatic art forms no exception to this law. What drama goes forth to discover and brings to light, is a deep-seated reality that is veiled from us, often in our own interests, by the necessities of life. What is this reality? What are these necessities? Poetry always expresses inward states. But amongst these states some arise mainly from contact with our fellow-men. They are the most intense as well as the most violent. As contrary electricities attract each other and accumulate between the two plates of the condenser from which the spark will presently flash, so, by simply bringing people together, strong attractions and repulsions take place, followed by an utter loss of balance, in a word, by that electrification of the soul known as passion. Were man to give way to the impulse of his natural feelings, were there neither social nor moral law, these outbursts of violent feeling would be the ordinary rule in life. But utility demands that these outbursts should be foreseen and averted. Man must live in society, and consequently submit to rules. And what interest advises, reason commands: duty calls, and we have to obey the summons. Under this dual influence has perforce been formed an outward layer of feelings and ideas which make for permanence, aim at becoming common to all men, and cover, when they are not strong enough to extinguish it, the inner fire of individual passions. The slow progress of mankind in the direction of an increasingly peaceful social life has gradually consolidated this layer, just as the life of our planet itself has been one long effort to cover over with a cool and solid crust the fiery mass of seething metals. But volcanic eruptions occur. And if the earth were a living being, as mythology has feigned, most likely when in repose it would take delight in dreaming of these sudden explosions, whereby it suddenly resumes possession of its innermost nature. Such is just the kind of pleasure that is provided for us by drama. Beneath the quiet humdrum life that reason and society have fashioned for us, it stirs something within us which luckily does not explode, but which it makes us feel in its inner tension. It offers nature her revenge upon society. Sometimes it makes straight for the goal, summoning up to the surface, from the depths below, passions that produce a general upheaval. Sometimes it effects a flank movement, as is often the case in contemporary drama; with a skill that is frequently sophistical, it shows up the inconsistencies of society; it exaggerates the shams and shibboleths of the social law; and so indirectly, by merely dissolving or corroding the outer crust, it again brings us back to the inner core. But, in both cases, whether it weakens society or strengthens nature, it has the same end in view: that of laying bare a secret portion of ourselves, – what might be called the tragic element in our character.

This is indeed the impression we get after seeing a stirring drama. What has just interested us is not so much what we have been told about others as the glimpse we have caught of ourselves – a whole host of ghostly feelings, emotions and events that would fain have come into real existence, but, fortunately for us, did not. It also seems as if an appeal had been made within us to certain ancestral memories belonging to a far-away past – memories so deep-seated and so foreign to our present life that this latter, for a moment, seems something unreal and conventional, for which we shall have to serve a fresh apprenticeship. So it is indeed a deeper reality that drama draws up from beneath our superficial and utilitarian attainments, and this art has the same end in view as all the others.

Hence it follows that art always aims at what is *individual*. What the artist fixes on his canvas is something he has seen at a certain spot, on a certain day, at a certain hour, with a colouring that will never be seen again. What the poet sings of is a certain mood which was his, and his alone, and which will never return. What the dramatist unfolds before us is the life-history of a soul, a living tissue of feelings and events – something, in short, which has once happened and can never be repeated. We may, indeed, give general names to these feelings, but they cannot be the same thing in another soul. They are *individualised*. Thereby, and thereby only, do they belong to art; for generalities, symbols or even types, form the current coin of our daily perception. How, then, does a misunderstanding on this point arise?

The reason lies in the fact that two very different things have been mistaken for each other: the generality of things and that of the opinions we come to regarding them. Because a feeling is generally recognised as true, it does not follow that it is a general feeling. Nothing could be more unique than the character of Hamlet. Though he may resemble other men in some respects, it is clearly not on that account that he interests us most. But he is universally accepted and regarded as a living character. In this sense only is he universally true. The same holds good of all the other products of art. Each of them is unique, and yet, if it bear the stamp of genius, it will come to be accepted by everybody. Why will it be accepted? And if it is unique of its kind, by what sign do we know it to be genuine? Evidently, by the very effort it forces us to make against our predispositions in order to see sincerely. Sincerity is contagious. What the artist has seen we shall probably never see again, or at least never see in exactly the same way; but if he has actually seen it, the attempt he has made to lift the veil compels our imitation. His work is an example which we take as a lesson. And the efficacy of the lesson is the exact standard of the genuineness of the work. Consequently, truth bears within itself a power of conviction, nay, of conversion, which is the sign that enables us to recognise it. The greater the work and the more profound the dimly apprehended truth, the longer may the effect be in coming, but, on the other hand, the more universal will that effect tend to become. So the universality here lies in the effect produced, and not in the cause.

Altogether different is the object of comedy. Here it is in the work itself that the generality lies. Comedy depicts characters we have already come across and shall meet with again. It takes note of similarities. It aims at placing types before our eyes. It even creates new types, if necessary. In this respect it forms a contrast to all the other arts.

The very titles of certain classical comedies are significant in themselves. Le Misanthrope, l'Avare, le Joueur, le Distrait, etc., are names of whole classes of people; and even when a character comedy has a proper noun as its title, this proper noun is speedily swept away, by the very weight of its contents, into the stream of common nouns. We say "a Tartuffe," but we should never say "a Phedre" or "a Polyeucte."

Above all, a tragic poet will never think of grouping around the chief character in his play secondary characters to serve as simplified copies, so to speak, of the former. The hero of a tragedy represents an individuality unique of its kind. It may be possible to imitate him, but then we shall be passing, whether consciously or not, from the tragic to the comic. No one is like him, because he is like no one. But a remarkable instinct, on the contrary, impels the comic poet, once he has elaborated his central character, to cause other characters, displaying the same general traits, to revolve as satellites round him. Many comedies have either a plural noun or some collective term as their title. "Les Femmes savantes," "Les Precieuses ridicules," "Le Monde ou l'on s'ennuie," etc., represent so many rallying points on the stage adopted by different groups of characters, all belonging to one identical type. It would be interesting to analyse this tendency in comedy. Maybe dramatists have caught a glimpse of a fact recently brought forward by mental pathology, viz. that cranks of the same kind are drawn, by a secret attraction, to seek each other's company. Without precisely coming within the province of medicine, the comic individual, as we have shown, is in some way absentminded, and the transition from absent-mindedness to crankiness is continuous. But there is also another reason. If the comic poet's object is to offer us types, that is to say, characters capable of self-

78

repetition, how can he set about it better than by showing us, in each instance, several different copies of the same model? That is just what the naturalist does in order to define a species. He enumerates and describes its main varieties.

This essential difference between tragedy and comedy, the former being concerned with individuals and the latter with classes, is revealed in yet another way. It appears in the first draft of the work. From the outset it is manifested by two radically different methods of observation.

Though the assertion may seem paradoxical, a study of other men is probably not necessary to the tragic poet. We find some of the great poets have lived a retiring, homely sort of life, without having a chance of witnessing around them an outburst of the passions they have so faithfully depicted. But, supposing even they had witnessed such a spectacle, it is doubtful whether they would have found it of much use. For what interests us in the work of the poet is the glimpse we get of certain profound moods or inner struggles. Now, this glimpse cannot be obtained from without. Our souls are impenetrable to one another. Certain signs of passion are all that we ever apperceive externally. These we interpret – though always, by the way, defectively – only by analogy with what we have ourselves experienced. So what we experience is the main point, and we cannot become thoroughly acquainted with anything but our own heart – supposing we ever get so far. Does this mean that the poet has experienced what he depicts, that he has gone through the various situations he makes his characters traverse, and lived the whole of their inner life? Here, too, the biographies of poets would contradict such a supposition. How, indeed, could the same man have been Macbeth, Hamlet, Othello, King Lear, and many others? But then a distinction should perhaps here be made between the personality *we have* and all those we might have had. Our character is the result of a choice that is continually being renewed. There are points – at all events there seem to be – all along the way, where we may branch off, and we perceive many possible directions though we are unable to take more than one. To retrace one's steps, and follow to the end the faintly distinguishable directions, appears to be the essential element in poetic imagination. Of course, Shakespeare was neither Macbeth, nor Hamlet, nor Othello; still, he *might have been* these several characters if the circumstances of the case on the one hand, and the consent of his will on the other, had caused to break out into explosive action what was nothing more than an inner prompting. We are strangely mistaken as to the part played by poetic imagination, if we think it pieces together its heroes out of fragments filched from right and left, as though it were patching together a harlequin's motley. Nothing living would result from that. Life cannot be recomposed; it can only be looked at and reproduced. Poetic imagination is but a fuller view of reality. If the characters created by a poet give us the impression of life, it is only because they are the poet himself, – multiplication or division of the poet, – the poet plumbing the depths of his own nature in so powerful an effort of inner observation that he lays hold of the potential in the real, and takes up what nature has left as a mere outline or sketch in his soul in order to make of it a finished work of art.

Altogether different is the kind of observation from which comedy springs. It is directed outwards. However interested a dramatist may be in the comic features of human nature, he will hardly go, I imagine, to the extent of trying to discover his own. Besides, he would not find them, for we are never ridiculous except in some point that remains hidden from our own consciousness. It is on others, then, that such observation must perforce be practised. But it; will, for this very reason, assume a character of generality that it cannot have when we apply it to ourselves. Settling on the surface, it will not be more than skin-deep, dealing with persons at the point at which they come into contact and become capable of resembling one another. It will go no farther. Even if it could, it would not desire to do so, for it would have nothing to gain in the process.

To penetrate too far into the personality, to couple the outer effect with causes that are too deep-seated, would mean to endanger and in the end to sacrifice all that was laughable in the effect. In order that we may be tempted to laugh at it, we must localise its cause in some intermediate region of the soul. Consequently, the effect must appear to us as an average effect, as expressing an average of mankind. And, like all averages, this one is obtained by bringing together scattered data, by comparing analogous cases and extracting their essence, in short by a process of abstraction and generalisation similar to that which the physicist brings to bear upon facts with the object of grouping them under laws. In a word, method and object are here of the same nature as in the inductive sciences, in that observation is always external and the result always general.

And so we come back, by a roundabout way, to the double conclusion we reached in the course of our investigations. On the one hand, a person is never ridiculous except through some mental attribute resembling absent-mindedness, through something that lives upon him without forming part of his organism, after the fashion of a parasite; that is the reason this state of mind is observable from without and capable of being corrected. But, on the other hand, just because laughter aims at correcting, it is expedient that the correction should reach as great a number of persons as possible. This is the reason comic observation instinctively proceeds to what is general. It chooses such peculiarities as admit of being reproduced and consequently are not indissolubly bound up with the individuality of a single person, – a possibly common sort of uncommonness, so to say, – peculiarities that are held in common. By transferring them to the stage, it creates works which doubtless belong to art in that their only visible aim is to please, but which will be found to contrast with other works of art by reason of their generality and also of their scarcely confessed or scarcely conscious intention to correct and instruct. So we were probably right in saying that comedy lies midway between art and life. It is not disinterested as genuine art is. By organis-ing laughter, comedy accepts social life as a natural environment, it even obeys an impulse of social life. And in this respect it turns its back upon art, which is a breaking away from society and a return to pure nature.

II

Now let us see, in the light of what has gone before, the line to take for creating an ideally comic type of character, comic in itself, in its origin, and in all its manifestations. It must be deep-rooted, so as to supply comedy with inexhaustible matter, and yet superficial, in order that it may remain within the scope of comedy; invisible to its actual owner, for the comic ever partakes of the unconscious, but visible to everybody else, so that it may call forth general laughter, extremely considerate to its own self, so that it may be displayed without scruple, but troublesome to others, so that they may repress it without pity; immediately repressible, so that our laughter may not have been wasted, but sure of reappearing under fresh aspects, so that laughter may always find something to do; inseparable from social life, although insufferable to society; capable – in order that it may assume the greatest imaginable variety of forms – of being tacked on to all the vices and even to a good many virtues. Truly a goodly number of elements to fuse together! But a chemist of the soul, entrusted with this elaborate preparation, would be somewhat disappointed when pouring out the contents of his retort. He would find he had taken a vast deal of trouble to compound a mixture which may be found ready-made and free of expense, for it is as widespread throughout mankind as air throughout nature.

This mixture is vanity. Probably there is not a single failing that is more superficial or more deep-rooted. The wounds it receives are never very serious, and yet they are seldom healed. The services rendered to it are the most unreal of all services, and yet they are the very ones that meet with lasting gratitude. It is scarcely a vice, and yet all the vices are drawn into its orbit and, in proportion as they become more refined and artificial, tend to be nothing more than a means of satisfying it. The outcome of social life, since it is an admiration of ourselves based on the admiration we think we are inspiring in others, it is even more natural, more universally innate than egoism; for egoism may be conquered by nature, whereas only by reflection do we get the better of vanity. It does not seem, indeed, as if men were ever born modest, unless we dub with the name of modesty a sort of purely physical bashfulness, which is nearer to pride than is generally supposed. True modesty can be nothing but a meditation on vanity. It springs from the sight of others' mistakes and the dread of being similarly deceived. It is a sort of scientific cautiousness with respect to what we shall say and think of ourselves. It is made up of improvements and aftertouches. In short, it is an acquired virtue.

It is no easy matter to define the point at which the anxiety to become modest may be distinguished from the dread of becoming ridiculous. But surely, at the outset, this dread and this anxiety are one and the same thing. A complete investigation into the illusions of vanity, and into the ridicule that clings to them, would cast a strange light upon the whole theory of laughter. We should find laughter performing, with mathematical regularity, one of its main functions – that of bringing back to complete self-consciousness a certain self-admiration which is almost automatic, and thus obtaining the greatest possible sociability of characters. We should see that vanity, though it is a natural product of social life, is an inconvenience to society, just as certain slight poisons, continually secreted by the human organism, would destroy it in the long run, if they were not neutralised by other secretions. Laughter is unceasingly doing work of this kind. In this respect, it might be said that the specific remedy for vanity is laughter, and that the one failing that is essentially laughable is vanity.

While dealing with the comic in form and movement, we showed how any simple image, laughable in itself, is capable of worming its way into other images of a more complex nature and instilling into them something of its comic essence; thus, the highest forms of the comic can sometimes be explained by the lowest. The inverse process, however, is perhaps even more common, and many coarse comic effects are the direct result of a drop from some very subtle comic element. For instance, vanity, that higher form of the comic, is an element we are prone to look for, minutely though unconsciously, in every manifestation of human activity. We look for it if only to laugh at it. Indeed, our imagination often locates it where it has no business to be. Perhaps we must attribute to this source the altogether coarse comic element in certain effects which psychologists have very inadequately explained by contrast: a short man bowing his head to pass beneath a large door; two individuals, one very tall the other a mere dwarf, gravely walking along arm-in-arm, etc. By scanning narrowly this latter image, we shall probably find that the shorter of the two persons seems as though he were trying *to raise himself* to the height of the taller, like the frog that wanted to make itself as large as the ox.

III

It would be quite impossible to go through all the peculiarities of character that either coalesce or compete with vanity in order to force themselves upon the attention of the comic poet. We have shown that all failings may become laughable, and even, occasionally, many a good quality. Even though a list of all the peculiarities that have ever been found ridiculous were drawn up, comedy would manage to add to them, not indeed by creating artificial ones, but by discovering lines of comic development that had hitherto gone unnoticed; thus does imagination isolate ever fresh figures in the intricate design of one and the same piece of tapestry. The essential condition, as we know, is that the peculiarity observed should straightway appear as a kind of *category* into which a number of individuals can step.

Now, there are ready-made categories established by society itself, and necessary to it because it is based on the division of labour. We mean the various trades, public services and professions. Each particular profession impresses on its corporate members certain habits of mind and peculiarities of character in which they resemble each other and also distinguish themselves from the rest. Small societies are thus formed within the bosom of Society at large. Doubtless they arise from the very organisation of Society as a whole. And yet, if they held too much aloof, there would be a risk of their proving harmful to sociability.

Now, it is the business of laughter to repress any separatist tendency. Its function is to convert rigidity into plasticity, to readapt the individual to the whole, in short, to round off the corners wherever they are met with. Accordingly, we here find a species of the comic whose varieties might be calculated beforehand. This we shall call the PROFESSIONAL COMIC.

Instead of taking up these varieties in detail, we prefer to lay stress upon what they have in common. In the forefront we find professional vanity. Each one of M. Jourdain's teachers exalts his own art above all the rest. In a play of Labiche there is a character who cannot understand how it is possible to be anything else than a timber merchant. Naturally he is a timber merchant himself. Note that vanity here tends to merge into *solemnity*, in proportion to the degree of quackery there is in the profession under consideration. For it is a remarkable fact that the more questionable an art, science or occupation is, the more those who practise it are inclined to regard themselves as invested with a kind of priesthood and to claim that all should bow before its mysteries. Useful professions are clearly meant for the public, but those whose utility is more dubious can only justify their existence by assuming that the public is meant for them: now, this is just the illusion that lies at the root of solemnity. Almost everything comic in Moliere's doctors comes from this source. They treat the patient as though he had been made for the doctors, and nature herself as an appendage to medicine.

Another form of this comic rigidity is what may be called *professional callousness*. The comic character is so tightly jammed into the rigid frame of his functions that he has no room to move or to be moved like other men. Only call to mind the answer Isabelle receives from Perrin Dandin, the judge, when she asks him how he can bear to look on when the poor wretches are being tortured: Bah! cela fait toujours passer une heure ou deux.[11]

Does not Tartuffe also manifest a sort of professional callousness when he says – it is true, by the mouth of Orgon: Et je verrais mourir frere, enfants, mere et femme, Que je m'en soucierais autant que de cela![12]

The device most in use, however, for making a profession ludicrous is to confine it, so to say, within the four corners of its own particular

---

11 Bah! it always helps to while away an hour or two.
12 Let brother, children, mother and wife all die, what should I care!

jargon. Judge, doctor and soldier are made to apply the language of law, medicine and strategy to the everyday affairs of life, as though they had became incapable of talking like ordinary people. As a rule, this kind of the ludicrous is rather coarse. It becomes more refined, however, as we have already said, if it reveals some peculiarity of character in addition to a professional habit. We will instance only Regnard's Joueur, who expresses himself with the utmost originality in terms borrowed from gambling, giving his valet the name of Hector, and calling his betrothed Pallas, du nom connu de la Dame de Pique; [13] or Moliere's Femmes savantes, where the comic element evidently consists largely in the translation of ideas of a scientific nature into terms of feminine sensibility: "Epicure me plait..." (Epicurus is charming), "J'aime les tourbillons" (I dote on vortices), etc. You have only to read the third act to find that Armande, Philaminte and Belise almost invariably express themselves in this style.

Proceeding further in the same direction, we discover that there is also such a thing as a professional logic, i.e. certain ways of reasoning that are customary in certain circles, which are valid for these circles, but untrue for the rest of the public. Now, the contrast between these two kinds of logic – one particular, the other universal – produces comic effects of a special nature, on which we may advantageously dwell at greater length. Here we touch upon a point of some consequence in the theory of laughter. We propose, therefore, to give the question a wider scope and consider it in its most general aspect.

IV

Eager as we have been to discover the deep-seated cause of the comic, we have so far had to neglect one of its most striking phenomena. We refer to the logic peculiar to the comic character and the comic group, a strange kind of logic, which, in some cases, may include a good deal of absurdity.

Theophile Gautier said that the comic in its extreme form was the logic of the absurd. More than one philosophy of laughter revolves round a like idea. Every comic effect, it is said, implies contradiction in some of its aspects. What makes us laugh is alleged to be the absurd realised in concrete shape, a "palpable absurdity"; – or, again, an apparent absurdity, which we swallow for the moment only to rectify it immediately afterwards; – or, better still, something absurd from one point of view though capable of a natural explanation from an-

13   Pallas, from the well-known name of the Queen of Spades.

other, etc. All these theories may contain some portion of the truth; but, in the first place, they apply only to certain rather obvious comic effects, and then, even where they do apply, they evidently take no account of the characteristic element of the laughable, that is, the *particular kind* of absurdity the comic contains when it does contain something absurd. Is an immediate proof of this desired? You have only to choose one of these definitions and make up effects in accordance with the formula: twice out of every three times there will be nothing laughable in the effect obtained. So we see that absurdity, when met with in the comic, is not absurdity *in general.* It is an absurdity of a definite kind. It does not create the comic; rather, we might say that the comic infuses into it its own particular essence. It is not a cause, but an effect – an effect of a very special kind, which reflects the special nature of its cause. Now, this cause is known to us; consequently we shall have no trouble in understanding the nature of the effect.

Assume, when out for a country walk, that you notice on the top of a hill something that bears a faint resemblance to a large motionless body with revolving arms. So far you do not know what it is, but you begin to search amongst your *ideas* – that is to say, in the present instance, amongst the recollections at your disposal – for that recollection which will best fit in with what you see. Almost immediately the image of a windmill comes into your mind: the object before you is a windmill. No matter if, before leaving the house, you have just been reading fairy-tales telling of giants with enormous arms; for although common sense consists mainly in being able to remember, it consists even more in being able to forget. Common sense represents the endeavour of a mind continually adapting itself anew and changing ideas when it changes objects. It is the mobility of the intelligence conforming exactly to the mobility of things. It is the moving continuity of our attention to life. But now, let us take Don Quixote setting out for the wars. The romances he has been reading all tell of knights encountering, on the way, giant adversaries. He therefore must needs encounter a giant. This idea of a giant is a privileged recollection which has taken its abode in his mind and lies there in wait, motionless, watching for an opportunity to sally forth and become embodied in a thing. It *is bent* on entering the material world, and so the very first object he sees bearing the faintest resemblance to a giant is invested with the form of one. Thus Don Quixote sees giants where we see windmills. This is comical; it is also absurd. But is it a mere absurdity, – an absurdity of an indefinite kind?

It is a very special inversion of common sense. It consists in seeking to mould things on an idea of one's own, instead of moulding one's ideas on things, – in seeing before us what we are thinking of, instead of thinking of what we see. Good sense would have us leave all our memories in their proper rank and file; then the appropriate memory will every time answer the summons of the situation of the moment and serve only to interpret it. But in Don Quixote, on the contrary, there is one group of memories in command of all the rest and dominating the character itself: thus it is reality that now has to bow to imagination, its only function being to supply fancy with a body. Once the illusion has been created, Don Quixote develops it logically enough in all its consequences; he proceeds with the certainty and precision of a somnambulist who is acting his dream. Such, then, is the origin of his delusions, and such the particular logic which controls this particular absurdity. Now, is this logic peculiar to Don Quixote?

We have shown that the comic character always errs through obstinacy of mind or of disposition, through absentmindedness, in short, through automatism. At the root of the comic there is a sort of rigidity which compels its victims to keep strictly to one path, to follow it straight along, to shut their ears and refuse to listen. In Moliere's plays how many comic scenes can be reduced to this simple type: *A character following up his one idea,* and continually recurring to it in spite of incessant interruptions! The transition seems to take place imperceptibly from the man who will listen to nothing to the one who will see nothing, and from this latter to the one who sees only what he wants to see. A stubborn spirit ends by adjusting things to its own way of thinking, instead of accommodating its thoughts to the things. So every comic character is on the highroad to the abovementioned illusion, and Don Quixote furnishes us with the general type of comic absurdity.

Is there a name for this inversion of common sense? Doubtless it may be found, in either an acute or a chronic form, in certain types of insanity. In many of its aspects it resembles a fixed idea. But neither insanity in general, nor fixed ideas in particular, are provocative of laughter: they are diseases, and arouse our pity.

Laughter, as we have seen, is incompatible with emotion. If there exists a madness that is laughable, it can only be one compatible with the general health of the mind, – a sane type of madness, one might say. Now, there is a sane state of the mind that resembles madness in every respect, in which we find the same associations of ideas as we do in lunacy, the same peculiar logic as in a fixed idea. This state is that of dreams. So either our analysis is incorrect, or it must be capable of being stated in the following theorem: Comic absurdity is of the same nature as that of dreams.

The behaviour of the intellect in a dream is exactly what we have just been describing. The mind, enamoured of itself, now seeks in the outer world nothing more than a pretext for realising its imaginations. A confused murmur of sounds still reaches the ear, colours enter the field of vision, the senses are not completely shut in. But the dreamer, instead of appealing to the whole of his recollections for the interpretation of what his senses perceive, makes use of what he perceives to give substance to the particular recollection he favours: thus, according to the mood of the dreamer and the idea that fills his imagination at the time, a gust of wind blowing down the chimney becomes the howl of a wild beast or a tuneful melody. Such is the ordinary mechanism of illusion in dreams.

Now, if comic illusion is similar to dream illusion, if the logic of the comic is the logic of dreams, we may expect to discover in the logic of the laughable all the peculiarities of dream logic. Here, again, we shall find an illustration of the law with which we are well acquainted: given one form of the laughable, other forms that are lacking in the same comic essence become laughable from their outward resemblance to the first. Indeed, it is not difficult to see that any *play of ideas* may afford us amusement if only it bring back to mind, more or less distinctly, the play of dreamland.

We shall first call attention to a certain general relaxation of the rules of reasoning. The reasonings at which we laugh are those we know to be false, but which we might accept as true were we to hear them in a dream. They counterfeit true reasoning just sufficiently to deceive a mind dropping off to sleep. There is still an element of logic in them, if you will, but it is a logic lacking in tension and, for that very reason, affording us relief from intellectual effort. Many "witticisms" are reasonings of this kind, considerably abridged reasonings, of which we are given only the beginning and the end. Such play upon ideas evolves in the direction of a play upon words in proportion as the relations set up between the ideas become more superficial: gradually we come to take no account of the meaning of the words we hear, but only of their sound. It might be instructive to compare with dreams certain comic scenes in which one of the characters systematically repeats in a nonsensical fashion what another character whispers in his ear. If you fall asleep with people talking round you, you sometimes find that what they say gradually becomes devoid of meaning, that the sounds get distorted, as it were, and recombine in a haphazard fashion to form in your mind the strangest of meanings, and that you are reproducing between yourself and the different speakers the scene between Petit-Jean and The Prompter.[14]

There are also *comic obsessions* that seem to bear a great resemblance to dream obsessions. Who has not had the experience of seeing the same image appear in several successive dreams, assuming a plausible meaning in each of them, whereas these dreams had no other point in common. Effects of repetition sometimes present this special form on the stage or in fiction: some of them, in fact, sound as though they belonged to a dream. It may be the same with the burden of many a song: it persistently recurs, always unchanged, at the end of every verse, each time with a different meaning.

Not infrequently do we notice in dreams a particular *crescendo*, a weird effect that grows more pronounced as we proceed. The first concession extorted from reason introduces a second; and this one, another of a more serious nature; and so on till the crowning absurdity is reached. Now, this progress towards the absurd produces on the dreamer a very peculiar sensation. Such is probably the experience of the tippler when he feels himself pleasantly drifting into a state of blankness in which neither reason nor propriety has any meaning for him. Now, consider whether some of Moliere's plays would not produce the same sensation: for instance, Monsieur de Pourceaugnac, which, after beginning almost reasonably, develops into a sequence of all sorts of absurdities. Consider also the Bourgeois gentilhomme, where the different characters seem to allow themselves to be caught up in a very whirlwind of madness as the play proceeds. "If it is possible to find a man more completely mad, I will go and publish it in Rome." This sentence, which warns us that the play is over, rouses us from the increasingly extravagant dream into which, along with M. Jourdain, we have been sinking.

But, above all, there is a special madness that is peculiar to dreams. There are certain special contradictions so natural to the imagination of a dreamer, and so absurd to the reason of a man wide-awake, that

---

14   Les Plaideurs (Racine).

it would be impossible to give a full and correct idea of their nature to anyone who had not experienced them. We allude to the strange fusion that a dream often effects between two persons who henceforth form only one and yet remain distinct. Generally one of these is the dreamer himself. He feels he has not ceased to be what he is; yet he has become someone else. He is himself, and not himself. He hears himself speak and sees himself act, but he feels that some other "he" has borrowed his body and stolen his voice. Or perhaps he is conscious of speaking and acting as usual, but he speaks of himself as a stranger with whom he has nothing in common; he has stepped out of his own self. Does it not seem as though we found this same extraordinary confusion in many a comic scene? I am not speaking of Amphitryon, in which play the confusion is perhaps suggested to the mind of the spectator, though the bulk of the comic effect proceeds rather from what we have already called a "reciprocal interference of two series." I am speaking of the extravagant and comic reasonings in which we really meet with this confusion in its pure form, though it requires some looking into to pick it out. For instance, listen to Mark Twain's replies to the reporter who called to interview him:

Q.   Isn't that a brother of yours?

A.   Oh! yes, yes, yes! Now you remind me of it, that was a brother of mine. That's William - Bill we called him. Poor old Bill!

Q.   Why? Is he dead, then?

A.   Ah! well, I suppose so. We never could tell. There was a great mystery about it.

Q.   That is sad, very sad. He disappeared, then?

A.   Well, yes, in a sort of general way. We buried him.

Q.   BURIED him! BURIED him, without knowing whether he was dead or not?

A.   Oh no! Not that. He was dead enough.

Q.   Well, I confess that I can't understand this. If you buried him, and you knew he was dead –

A.   No! no! We only thought he was.

Q.   Oh, I see! He came to life again?

A.   I bet he didn't.

Q.   Well, I never heard anything like this. somebody was dead. somebody was buried. Now, where was the mystery?

A.   Ah! that's just it! That's it exactly. You see, we were twins, – defunct and I, – and we got mixed in the bath-tub when we were only two weeks old, and one of us was drowned. But we didn't know which. Some think it was Bill. Some think it was me.

Q.   Well, that is remarkable. What do you think?

A.   Goodness knows! I would give whole worlds to know. This solemn, this awful tragedy has cast a gloom over my whole life. But I will tell you a secret now, which I have never revealed to any creature before. One of us had a peculiar mark, – a large mole on the back of his left hand: that was ME. *That child was the one that was drowned!* ... *etc., etc.*

A close examination will show us that the absurdity of this dialogue is by no means an absurdity of an ordinary type. It would disappear were not the speaker himself one of the twins in the story. It results entirely from the fact that Mark Twain asserts he is one of these twins, whilst all the time he talks as though he were a third person who tells the tale. In many of our dreams we adopt exactly the same method.

V

Regarded from this latter point of view, the comic seems to show itself in a form somewhat different from the one we lately attributed to it. Up to this point, we have regarded laughter as first and foremost a means of correction. If you take the series of comic varieties and isolate the predominant types at long intervals, you will find that all the intervening varieties borrow their comic quality from their resemblance to these types, and that the types themselves are so many models of impertinence with regard to society. To these impertinences society retorts by laughter, an even greater impertinence. So evidently there is nothing very benevolent in laughter. It seems rather inclined to return evil for evil.

But this is not what we are immediately struck by in our first impression of the laughable. The comic character is often one with whom, to begin with, our mind, or rather our body, sympathises. By this is meant that we put ourselves for a very short time in his place, adopt his gestures, words, arid actions, and, if amused by anything laughable in him, invite him, in imagination, to share his amusement with us; in fact, we treat him first as a playmate. So, in the laugher we find a "hail-fel-low-well-met" spirit – as far, at least, as appearances go – which it would be wrong of us not to take into consideration. In particular, there is in laughter a movement of relaxation which has often been noticed, and the reason of which we must try to discover. Nowhere is this impression more noticeable than in the last few examples. In them, indeed, we shall find its explanation.

When the comic character automatically follows up his idea, he ultimately thinks, speaks and acts as though he were dreaming. Now, a dream is a relaxation. To remain in touch with things and men, to see nothing but what is existent and think nothing but what is consis-tent, demands a continuous effort of intellectual tension. This effort is common sense. And to remain sensible is, indeed, to remain at work. But to detach oneself from things and yet continue to perceive images, to break away from logic and yet continue to string together ideas, is to indulge in play or, if you prefer, in dolce far niente. So, comic ab-surdity gives us from the outset the impression of playing with ideas. Our first impulse is to join in the game. That relieves us from the strain of thinking. Now, the same might be said of the other forms of the laughable. Deep-rooted in the comic, there is always a tendency, we said, to take the line of least resistance, generally that of habit. The comic character no longer tries to be ceaselessly adapting and readapt-ing himself to the society of which he is a member. He slackens in the attention that is due to life. He more or less resembles the absentmind-ed. Maybe his will is here even more concerned than his intellect, and there is not so much a want of attention as a lack of tension; still, in some way or another, he is absent, away from his work, taking it easy. He abandons social convention, as indeed – in the case we have just been considering – he abandoned logic. Here, too, our first impulse is to accept the invitation to take it easy. For a short time, at all events, we join in the game. And that relieves us from the strain of living.

But we rest only for a short time. The sympathy that is capable of entering into the impression of the comic is a very fleeting one. It also comes from a lapse in attention. Thus, a stern father may at times forget himself and join in some prank his child is playing, only to check him-self at once in order to correct it.

Laughter is, above all, a corrective. Being intended to humiliate, it must make a painful impression on the person against whom it is di-rected. By laughter, society avenges itself for the liberties taken with it. It would fail in its object if it bore the stamp of sympathy or kindness.

Shall we be told that the motive, at all events; may be a good one, that we often punish because we love, and that laughter, by checking the outer manifestations of certain failings, thus causes the person laughed at to correct these failings and thereby improve himself inwardly?

Much might be said on this point. As a general rule, and speaking roughly, laughter doubtless exercises a useful function. Indeed, the whole of our analysis points to this fact. But it does not therefore follow that laughter always hits the mark or is invariably inspired by sentiments of kindness or even of justice.

To be certain of always hitting the mark, it would have to proceed from an act of reflection. Now, laughter is simply the result of a mechanism set up in us by nature or, what is almost the same thing, by our long acquaintance with social life. It goes off spontaneously and returns tit for tat. It has no time to look where it hits. Laughter punishes certain failing's somewhat as disease punishes certain forms of excess, striking down some who are innocent and sparing some who are guilty, aiming at a general result and incapable of dealing separately with each individual case. And so it is with everything that comes to pass by natural means instead of happening by conscious reflection. An average of justice may show itself in the total result, though the details, taken separately, often point to anything but justice.

In this sense, laughter cannot be absolutely just. Nor should it be kind-hearted either. Its function is to intimidate by humiliating. Now, it would not succeed in doing this, had not nature implanted for that very purpose, even in the best of men, a spark of spitefulness or, at all events, of mischief. Perhaps we had better not investigate this point too closely, for we should not find anything very flattering to ourselves. We should see that this movement of relaxation or expansion is nothing but a prelude to laughter, that the laugher immediately retires within himself, more self-assertive and conceited than ever, and is evidently disposed to look upon another's personality as a marionette of which he pulls the strings. In this presumptuousness we speedily discern a degree of egoism and, behind this latter, something less spontaneous and more bitter, the beginnings of a curious pessimism which becomes the more pronounced as the laugher more closely analyses his laughter.

Here, as elsewhere, nature has utilised evil with a view to good. It is more especially the good that has engaged our attention throughout this work. We have seen that the more society improves, the more plastic is the adaptability it obtains from its members; while the greater the tendency towards increasing stability below, the more does it force to the surface the disturbing elements inseparable from so vast a bulk; and thus laughter performs a useful function by emphasising the form of these significant undulations. Such is also the truceless warfare of the waves on the surface of the sea, whilst profound peace reigns in the depths below. The billows clash and collide with each other, as they strive to find their level. A fringe of snow-white foam, feathery and frolicsome, follows their changing outlines. From time to time, the receding wave leaves behind a remnant of foam on the sandy beach. The child, who plays hard by, picks up a handful, and, the next moment, is astonished to find that nothing remains in his grasp but a few drops of water, water that is far more brackish, far more bitter than that of the wave which brought it. Laughter comes into being in the self-same fashion. It indicates a slight revolt on the surface of social life. It instantly adopts the changing forms of the disturbance. It, also, is afroth with a saline base. Like froth, it sparkles. It is gaiety itself. But the philosopher who gathers a handful to taste may find that the substance is scanty, and the after-taste bitter.

THE END

℘

CPSIA information can be obtained
at www.ICGtesting.com
Printed in the USA
BVOW03s1931150817
492141BV00001B/74/P

9 781604 501063

www.ArcManor.com

ISBN 978-1-60450-106-3

O9-BRW-783